BIRDS OF BRITAIN AND EUROPE

Birds of Britain & Europe *IN COLOUR*

Dennis Avon & Tony Tilford
Foreword and Introduction by
Jim Flegg

BLANDFORD

This edition first published in the UK 1989
by Blandford Press,
an imprint of Cassell plc
Artillery House, Artillery Row,
London, SW1P 1RT

Originally published in 1975
Reprinted in 1978

British Library Cataloguing in Publication Data
Avon, Denis
Birds of Britain and Europe
1. Europe. Birds
I. Title II. Tilford, Tony
598.294

ISBN 0-7137-2067-0

Printed and bound by Graficromo, Spain

Contents

(For alphabetical Species Index see page 174)

Foreword

Of all their attractions the universal presence of birds around us must be one of the greatest. We can gain continuous enjoyment from their presence but do we, in fact, derive as much benefit as we might from the interest that wild birds have to offer?

While all of us may *look* at birds, we need help if we are to watch and identify them and understand their actions: how much greater becomes the enjoyment as our knowledge and watching skills increase. This is the vital assistance that this book provides, beyond its intrinsic fascination. Birds provide excellent examples of natural history in action. They are an educational aid available to all, a spectrum of living ecology far removed from textbooks.

In our technological age when the potential effects of industrial developments on the environment are unknown in advance birds can serve as an early-warning system for impending upsets in environmental balance, so a widespread awareness and understanding of birds is for man's general good. Equally, such an understanding of birds as representatives of the creatures and plants that share our environment may go a long way towards augmenting our fragmentary network of nature reserves by providing large areas of hospitable countryside where they may be free of persecution and pollution.

For centuries, birdwatchers had to rely on the skill with pen and brush of wild-life artists to provide guides to birds. There followed the era of black-and-white photography, often of great technical excellence but all too often centred on photography at the nest – a situation where few people will see their birds anyway. Dennis Avon and Tony Tilford have developed colour photographic techniques to an extraordinary degree enabling them to produce these magnificent photographs of birds in everyday action against normal surroundings – a great aid to identification. Not only that, but the insight and knowledge of birds gained in the process have enabled them to show with great clarity how the bird functions in its own environment, both by the illustrations and by the wealth of text notes that augment them. Authors, printers and publishers are to be congratulated and thanked for producing such an attractive, worthwhile and educative guide to our birds.

Jim Flegg

ACKNOWLEDGEMENTS

It would be impossible to compile a book of this nature without the help of innumerable people and without referring to other published works. The list of helpers is really too long to include so we hope they will appreciate that their anonymity in no way reflects ingratitude on the part of the authors.

We particularly wish to thank Jim Flegg for writing the Foreword and Introduction and for his guidance and invaluable comments on the text. Our thanks go also to Clive Minton and the Wash Wader Ringing Group for up-to-date information on the Waders.

We wish to thank the Royal Society for the Protection of Birds and the Association of Natural History Photographic Societies for allowing us to use extracts from the Nature Photographers' Code of Practice in the section dealing with bird photography.

Our thanks are also due to Ardea Photographics for supplying the photographs by I. R. Beames, R. J. C. Blewitt and J. B. & S. Bottomley on pages 25, 51 and 173 respectively.

The quality of our photography is attributable to the excellent materials and equipment made by Kodak Ltd. and Canon Inc. Japan and we wish to thank them for the superb results these have given us.

Dennis Avon

Tony Tilford

Introduction

The Developing Awareness of Birds Man has always been interested in birds – the ancients regarded them as gods (and indeed remote communities still do); hunted with them (falcons are shown on Pharaoh's wrist); were mystified by their migrations. In the nineteenth century, ladies wore their feathers (causing great slaughter and the foundation of the conservation movement) and gentlemen shot them for their collections of stuffed specimens (few households were without the awful glass case) or collected their eggs with an enthusiasm that is today, fortunately, directed more towards stamps and train numbers.

The twentieth century has seen the dawn of a new interest in birds – alive and in their natural surroundings – for their intrinsic interest and beauty. Science has also benefited: in no other field have 'amateurs' contributed more to all aspects of study, leading the field in many cases. Today, with birds recognised as being indicators of the health of the environment, the birdwatcher's interest is in assessing numbers, discovering the life-history, productivity and mortality, migration routes and habitat preferences of birds. This has immense value for the community – losing none of its interest thereby! It was to foster co-operative studies of this nature that the British Trust for Ornithology was founded in 1932 – nearly half a century later, it has never been so enthusiastically involved.

Here, surely, lies the fascination of birds: they are always around us, always interesting – deep in the concrete canyons of the city or away on the remote rocky islets off our coasts.

Identification Bird identification can only be *taught* in small measure; it is a skill, and *practice* is the only way to acquire it. While the birds illustrated on these pages may seem very distinct, remember that often you will get much more fleeting views, perhaps of birds in flight. This is the time that a store of knowledge of the *way* a bird flies, walks (or runs or hops) and feeds is so valuable. All these features and the bird's general attitudes are combined by birdwatchers in a term 'jizz' and once familiarity has taught you the jizz of a particular species, you are unlikely to make mistakes over it again.

Of course field guides and sound recordings help, but nothing like so much as experience, particularly with a knowledgeable birdwatching friend to guide you round the pitfalls. To get good views of birds, you need good fieldcraft. Astonishing numbers of birdwatchers have no idea how much they miss by being hasty and noisy. Remember that birds sight and hearing are far better than ours (although they cannot smell) and try a few 'Red Indian' tricks to get closer to them. Move quietly; avoid chattering, coughing and laughter. Avoid brightly coloured clothes; keep close to sheltering cover and pause regularly to look and listen to what is going on. If you can hear a bird ahead try and sneak up on it; don't expose yourself on the skyline, or your shadow on water.

Most importantly, of course, choose and use a sensible pair of binoculars. Always try before buying, and go for moderate magnification ($\times 8 - \times 10$); a good field of view; good light transmission (object glass diameter 30–50 mm – the bigger the better); and glasses that sit easily in your hand, the controls at your finger-tips, and which do not weigh too much.

Topography of a Bird When attempting to identify a bird it is useful to know the terms relating to various parts of its body, particularly if you are making or comparing notes. The diagram illustrates all of the parts mentioned in this book and it is worth while memorising the terms used.

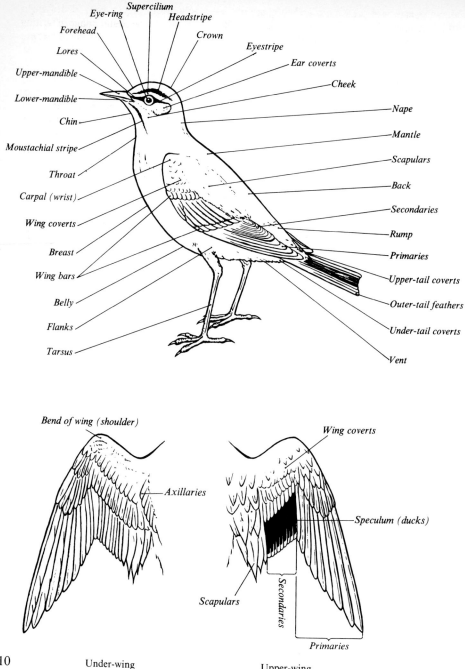

Supercilium
Eye-ring
Headstripe
Forehead
Crown
Lores
Eyestripe
Upper-mandible
Ear coverts
Lower-mandible
Cheek
Chin
Nape
Moustachial stripe
Mantle
Throat
Scapulars
Carpal (wrist)
Back
Wing coverts
Secondaries
Breast
Rump
Wing bars
Primaries
Belly
Upper-tail coverts
Flanks
Outer-tail feathers
Tarsus
Under-tail coverts
Vent

Bend of wing (shoulder)

Wing coverts

Axillaries

Speculum (ducks)

Scapulars

Secondaries

Primaries

10   Under-wing   Upper-wing

Call Notes and Song Call notes and song are often the only means of positively identifying a bird particularly if it is in thick cover. It is most difficult to convey the sound image in writing as bird calls are seldom similar to the human voice. The songs and calls written in the text are simplified phonetics and should be used only as a rough guide to the actual sound.

Order of Families So that zoologists, and especially ornithologists, of all nationalities may understand which bird is being talked about, a system of scientific names based on Latin or Greek (or a hybrid of both) is used. This was invented by the Swede Linnaeus many years ago. Obviously it is much more practical too, if similar birds are grouped together – and at several levels of relationship: thus the warbler **family** – the *Sylviidae* – contains several sub-groups, each called a **genus** and each genus contains one or usually more closely related **species**. Perhaps this is most easily understood with an example:

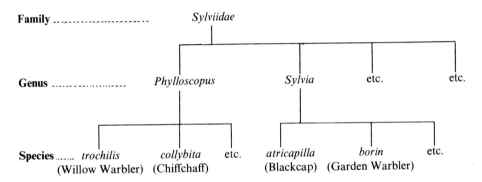

Zoologists who make special studies of the anatomy behaviour and evolution of birds, and who then decide how to classify them, are called taxonomists and systematists, and although they disagree quite often on details, the following list of European families is generally acceptable. It starts with those families considered to be the most primitive (the divers and the grebes) and progresses steadily to the sparrows, starlings and crows, which are considered to be the most highly evolved birds.

Divers *Gaviidae*
Grebes *Podicipitidae*
Petrels *Procellariidae*
Pelicans *Pelecanidae*
Gannets *Sulidae*
Cormorants and Shags *Phalacrocoracidae*
Herons *Ardeidae*
Storks *Ciconiidae*
Spoonbills *Plataleidae*
Flamingos *Phoenicopteridae*
Ducks, Geese, Swans *Anatidae*
Vultures, Eagles, Harriers, Hawks
 Accipitridae
Ospreys *Pandionidae*
Falcons *Falconidae*

Grouse and Ptarmigan *Tetraonidae*
Partridges, Quails, Pheasants *Phasianidae*
Button-Quails *Turnicidae*
Cranes *Gruidae*
Rails, Moorhens, Coots *Rallidae*
Bustards *Otididae*
Stone-curlews *Burhinidae*
Oystercatchers *Haematopodidae*
Lapwings, Plovers, Turnstones *Charadriidae*
Snipe, Curlews, Godwits, Sandpipers
 Scolopacidae
Avocets, Stilts *Recurvirostridae*
Phalaropes *Phalaropodidae*
Pratincoles *Glareolidae*
Skuas *Stercorariidae*

11

Gulls, Terns *Laridae*
Auks, *Alcidae*
Sandgrouse *Pteroclidae*
Pigeons and Doves *Columbidae*
Cuckoos *Cuculidae*
Barn Owls *Tytonidae*
Owls *Strigidae*
Nightjars *Caprimulgidae*
Swifts *Apodidae*
Kingfishers *Alcedinidae*
Bee-eaters *Meropidae*
Rollers *Coraciidae*
Hoopoes *Upupidae*
Woodpeckers, Wrynecks *Picidae*
Larks *Alaudidae*
Swallows and Martins *Hirundinidae*
Pipits, Wagtails *Motacillidae*
Shrikes *Laniidae*
Waxwings *Bombycillidae*

Dippers *Cinclidae*
Wrens *Troglodytidae*
Accentors *Prunellidae*
Thrushes, Wheatears, Chats, Redstarts, Nightingales, Robins *Turdidae*
Bearded Tits *Panuridae*
Warblers, Goldcrests *Sylviidae*
Flycatchers *Muscicapidae*
Tits *Paridae*
Nuthatches *Sittidae*
Tree Creepers *Certhiidae*
Buntings *Emberizidae*
Finches, Linnets, Redpolls, Crossbills *Fringillidae*
Sparrows and Snow Finches *Passeridae*
Starlings *Sturnidae*
Orioles *Oriolidae*
Ravens, Crows, Magpies, Jays *Corvidae*

Geographical Races Although one of the major features of birds is their extremely high mobility, the birdwatcher should not forget that some species are sedentary, and can be isolated by the nature of their surroundings, developing sometimes distinct plumages, sometimes distinct songs in the relatively inbred situation that this isolation produces. Thus in a journey across Europe, the Chaffinches will not all look, or sound, the same as those at the starting point, although in any one area, all Chaffinches seem alike. These localised forms are called **races**, or **subspecies**.

There is also a biological 'law' that says that the further north a particular species occurs, in general, the larger it is. Thus the Wheatears of Greenland are noticeably larger than those of Britain and Ireland – a feature that stands them in good stead, not just for survival in the colder region, but also because they must perform a longer migration. This is another way in which subspecies (or races) can be formed. With migrants, of course it does not matter if they mix, large and small, in the wintering area, so long as each race returns to its point of origin when the breeding season comes.

Migration Each year, for a couple of midsummer months after the snow has thawed, the Arctic tundra produces an amazing abundance of flowers. Equally amazing is the mass of insect life that flourishes in this brief spell, having survived the long winter as eggs or larvae. Further south, in temperate latitudes, we all know that in terms of insects and fruits, our countries are far richer in summer than during the winter, while in the tropics the lush fruitfulness – and the burdens of high insect populations – continue year-round. It is often said that nature abhors a vacuum, and it would be strange indeed if this brief period of temperate and arctic richness was not exploited. Birds are really the only group of animals mobile enough and fast enough to do this, and thus, over millennia, regular migration patterns have become established.

Perhaps the best examples of migration can be drawn in generalised form from amongst the waders. Wintering in southern Africa, they begin the northward flight in late March and April. There is a sense of urgency about the trip, and at the staging posts, flocks feed feverishly, fattening up – indeed storing away fat as 'fuel' for the next long flight stage. This is why the lakes, marshes and estuaries which are used on migration routes are of such vital importance, for without them the journey just could not be made. The sense of urgency stems from the shortness of the Arctic summer; birds must arrive in peak condition, nest and lay eggs shortly after arrival, hatch and raise their families before winter begins to close in again in August! Then the long journey begins again, often taken at a more leisurely pace moving southwards. The Arctic Tern is another example: breeding near the Arctic Circle, and 'wintering' off the Antarctic pack ice, it lives its life in maximum daylength as it moves from one hemisphere's summer to the other. This is only at the cost of a round trip of 25,000 miles or more – and as many terns will live for over twenty years, they have a high life mileage.

Clearly the undoubted hazards of these migratory journeys – the dangers of storms, getting blown off course, running the gauntlet of hunters in country after country, have been shown in evolutionary terms to be worth it so far as the species is concerned, and evolution is concerned with the fate of the species as a whole, not the individual.

But how do we find out about these things? Early this century, the technique of fixing a numbered metal ring to the bird's leg was developed, and now, each year, many hundreds of thousands of birds are ringed in Europe. The ring is very light in weight (about 250 of the smallest weigh as much as a 10p piece) and has a serial number – just like a car registration plate – stamped on it together with an address (usually a zoo or museum in the capital city) for its return when found. This address is important, as it must be equally understood by people as far apart as, say, a Brazilian fisherman or a hunting African in Zaire.

Birds are caught, either at the network of bird observatories spread across Europe, situated at good migration spots on the coast or in mountain passes, or by birdwatchers who have specially trained as ringers. In Britain, ringing is organised by the British Trust for Ornithology, and about 1,300 ringers handle 500,000 birds each year, of which some 12,000–14,000 are reported from all over the world: waders in the Arctic, ducks almost in China, shearwaters in Brazil, Swallows in South Africa, Kittiwakes in the U.S.A., terns in Australia!

Of course, most garden birds do not travel on this scale, but ringing can tell us that they move only a short distance from their birthplace in their lives, how long they live, and what causes their deaths, all vital pieces of information if we are to develop soundly based plans for conservation.

Adaptations   Throughout this book, you will see examples of how one or more organs have, in the course of evolution, become developed to a highly specialised degree, associated with the way of life, and especially the feeding techniques of the particular species. It is worth drawing some general conclusions on the types of legs, feet and bills and how they are used.

The birds of prey (usually fast, agile flyers – but note that owls rely on stealth) are equipped with astonishingly long legs and sharply hooked talons on strong toes. The length of leg is less surprising when you consider that the prey must be seized, in flight or on the ground, without the wings getting tangled up in the operation. They are flesh-eaters, so it is no surprise to find a strong, sharp, hooked bill ideal for tearing off lumps of flesh.

Most water-birds have webbed feet for swimming, but the auks use their rather stiff wings to swim under water, although they also have webbed feet. Others, like the herons, have rather longer legs than most so that they may exploit the food supply in deeper water. The Heron, the Moorhen and most waders have long toes, spreading the load and preventing the bird sinking into the mud. Many ducks filter food particles from mud in their rather spoon-like bills, while waders probe with bills of different lengths and strengths at varying depths for their favourite worms or shellfish – sometimes quite subtle differences in structure will ensure   13 ecological separation and prevent competition for the same food source between species: compare the Oystercatcher and the godwit, for example. Birds that feed on fish and slippery creatures show still more strangely adapted features: the Heron stabs, but also has a special comb-like claw to scrape scale off its feathers; the Merganser, a duck, has a bill with a serrated edge to grip its prey, the Puffin has projections like shark's teeth on the roof of its mouth for the same purpose; finally the Osprey, using its feet like all birds of prey, has its toes covered in a skin as prickly and rough as emery paper so that it doesn't drop its catch.

Smaller birds, too, are adapted to their way of life, although generally their legs and feet are in many ways similar (the woodpeckers are an exception, with specially developed toes and claws and a stiffened tail which serves as a 'prop'.) The insect-eaters can be recognised by their fine, needle-sharp bills, ideal for extracting eggs or larvae from crevices in plants. Those that take larger invertebrates, like worms, have correspondingly stouter bills – the thrushes are good examples. How different are the seed-eaters: all have stronger, wedge-shaped bills for crushing the seed to extract the nutritious kernel, but they range from the fine-pointed Goldfinch, extracting seeds from thistles and teazles, to the massive Hawfinch, crushing cherry and damson stones in its hefty bill.

Ethics in Birdwatching Despite the fact that many European countries have laws protecting birds, to the birdwatcher a code of ethics must always come first, as this will almost always be stricter than the law and a far better safeguard to the birds. Such a code can be summarised very simply:

ALWAYS PUT THE BIRDS' INTERESTS FIRST

There are any number of times when this simple instruction should be remembered, but perhaps the most important are at any stage in the nesting season and when the birds under observation are tired, perhaps newly arrived, immigrants, desperate for food and sleep.

Never deliberately disturb birds unless it is absolutely necessary to get a flight view; they will move in due course, and you will get far better views before they do. Similarly, when *you* have finished watching, don't just stand up and walk off. Somebody else may be watching too! Remember that large numbers of birdwatchers, quite understandably, like seeing a rare bird: *think* before you tell others of any discovery – can the bird be watched without disturbance, without damage to the surrounding habitat, without trespass on private property? The law often specially protects rare breeding birds – so should you. If you find a rare bird breeding, get confirmation from an absolutely trustworthy expert if you feel it necessary, but tell nobody else until after the breeding season, and remember that the birds may return in subsequent years. In extreme cases, it may be advisable to contact a national protection society such as Britain's Royal Society for the Protection of Birds (R.S.P.B.), and allow them to take any necessary measures.

Protection by Law In many countries, all or many species may be protected for some or all of the year. In most countries, game birds may only be taken in specified seasons, and only listed pest species can be killed by authorised persons at any time. Much the same protection applies to nests and eggs, and in Britain even disturbance of the breeding bird by close approach is prohibited for a range of specially protected species.

Birdwatchers of all nationalities should familiarise themselves with the bird protection laws of their own countries, and of those they intend to visit.

Despite the present-day interest in birds over much of Europe, there are still problems. 'Sportsmen' still shoot indiscriminately at anything that moves, some game-keepers will use traps or poison in mistaken attempts to eliminate birds of prey (which have their vital place in maintaining the balance of nature) and collectors still covet clutches of eggs – which once collected may be admired only in secret, coloured but lifeless shells of calcium carbonate instead of living, colourful birds.

To counter these pressures there are local and national conservation or protection societies, of which the largest is Britain's Royal Society for the Protection of Birds. Besides acting as a lobby to improve the law, and to enforce the existing ones, they maintain reserves protecting special habitats or species and strive, through education, to promote a greater awareness of environmental problems.

Nest-boxes and Bird-Tables One of the most rewarding and interesting ways of getting closer to birds, and even becoming involved in their family life, is to bring *them* to *you*. In winter, this is quite easily done for a wide range of species, even in urban surroundings. Put out bread close to the house, and you will tempt several species: Starlings and sparrows certainly, but both gulls and Reed Buntings will come to bread in cold weather! Increase the variety of food – add fruit, nuts and (vitally) water – and vary the way it is presented, some on the ground, some hanging, and many of the species in your neighbourhood may visit you. Much remains to be discovered about artificial food preferences: only recently have we discovered how much Siskins enjoy peanuts late in winter – but *why* in *red* plastic holders?

At its simplest, a nest-box is a hollow cube of roughly 150 mm side, with (for tits) an entrance hole just over 25 mm in diameter or one side half open (for Robins and Spotted Flycatchers). Clearly, for larger birds those dimensions will alter, but – perhaps irritatingly – the quality of the carpentry seems to have little influence on the intending users! There are a few do's and dont's:

(i) A removable lid makes the box more interesting and more educational – but do not over-visit, especially during nestbuilding and when the eggs are hatching or the young large. Use hooks to keep the lid shut.

(ii) Boxes should not be too close together – say 20 m apart.

(iii) They should have waterproof tops and drainage holes in the bottom.

(iv) Positioning is important: they should not be exposed to any climatic extremes – full sunlight, wind or beating rain.

(v) Height – boxes will be occupied from 1 to 10 m – more important is, can it be reached by predatory cats or squirrels, or by inquisitive small boys?

(vi) If cats may be a problem, protect the box by tying sprays of gorse round the trunk.

(vii) Clean out all nest-boxes at the end of the season.

(viii) Make necessary repairs *before* the spring.

The bibliography gives details of a guide-book for nest-box construction; there are numerous tempting possibilities for all birdwatchers, not just the competent carpenters amongst them, from a balsa-wood-filled box designed to attract woodpeckers (which excavate their own cavity), to floating 'islands' in gravel-pits – rafts with a topping of pebbles or plants on which water-birds will regularly nest!

Parasites Birds, like all vertebrates, have their problems with internal parasites, tapeworms, roundworms and flukes. Only occasionally do these build up to sufficient levels to cause fatalities in adult birds, but much remains to be discovered of their harmful impact on nestlings and recently fledged juveniles. Those parasites that live on the 'outside' of their host are called ectoparasites, and birds carry some ectoparasites with fascinating life-cycles. The louse-flies (*Hippoboscidae*) for example, are blood-suckers and remarkably adapted to life under the 15 feathers. They are flattened top-to-bottom and crab-like in shape, with strong hooked feet and the ability to move sideways with great speed to avoid bill or claw of the bird when it is preening. Yet another adaptation to parasitic life is the compression of the normal insect larval stages: the egg develops into a larva within the female, and the larval stages progress through to pupation (still within the female) until the pupa itself is laid. From this hatches a winged adult, which flies off to seek a new host. Swifts and House Martins often carry a heavy burden of louse-flies.

Nests, of course, are ideal sites for fleas, especially if they are in cavities and used year after year, as are Kingfisher burrows, woodpecker holes and nest-boxes if they are not cleaned out at the end of the season. Fleas are also blood-suckers, but in this case flattened from side-to-side to ease movement through feathers! Ticks and mites also find the nest the most convenient place for transfer from one host individual to another.

Another group of insects, the feather lice (*Mallophaga*) specialise as their name suggests in feeding on the feathers themselves, and on skin, blood and lymph. They, too, are specialised in structure with the strong gripping feet of the other parasites, and a flattened and elongate body. So specialised are they to their particular host's feather structure that the bird can often be placed accurately in its genus or even species by a taxonomist who has examined its feather lice without seeing the bird itself!

Man's Birds Relatively few birds have been domesticated for food purposes – the chicken and turkey, duck and goose are the prime examples. Perhaps this reflects the difficulty in restraining and taming creatures with the power of flight and often with an inbuilt seasonal immigration pattern. A counter to this argument is the wide range of species kept in cages and aviaries for man's pleasure – but this is a relatively recent development. Many of these birds, especially the seed-eaters, will thrive in captivity and breed freely. Nevertheless it *is* captivity, and those intending to keep birds must bear this in mind when constructing aviaries, in the same way that they should remember the often barbarous catching techniques and high mortality that takes place before colourful tropical birds reach the care that aviculturalists in temperate climes lavish on their charges.

Occasionally such birds escape, of course, and if sufficiently hardy, set up feral populations, sometimes to the detriment of native species, but more often not. For example, with a recent series of mild winters 'wild' populations of parakeets, budgerigars and several colourful ducks and pheasants are surviving. Other birds are deliberately released to augment native populations – fundamentally a much more dangerous experiment and in the opinion of most biologists, one to be discouraged. Rabbits and goats are the prime examples of the potential dangers, but the Little Owl (liberated in the British Isles as late as last century), Mute Swan, Canada Goose, Red-legged Partridge and Pheasant are now successful European residents without, apparently, causing severe disruption of the existing bird communities.

It is no surprise to find that so many of these are 'game' birds and are hunted, usually with guns but occasionally with falcons, for a combination of food and sport – now largely sport as the dietary necessity has been removed. Game is a term embracing most ducks, several geese and several waders, besides the grain-eating pheasants, partridges and related grouse species. Birdwatchers will often encounter high densities of some of these species, maintained with the protection of game-keepers and with artificial food supplies to produce larger numbers for the guns when the shooting season opens. Fortunately shooting associations maintain unshot refuges and often do enormous good in terms of habitat development and management, so that a wide range of birds besides game may benefit from their conservation activities.

Jim Flegg

Distribution Maps

The distribution maps accompanying the species notes have been compiled from the most up-to-date information available to the authors. It is impossible to draw precise maps since factors such as climatic change affect the distribution over the years. Owing to the small scale of the maps, the areas shown cover many types of habitat and it is important to realise that any bird will usually be found only in a suitable habitat. In some cases, such as for coastal birds, the area of tone on the map has been exaggerated in order to render it easily visible. However, reference to the notes will give some indication as to the type of habitat where one can expect to find the bird.

The grey tone denotes the area in which a bird species normally breeds – and the red tone the area where the majority are known to spend the winter.

Where red and grey tones overlap, birds of the species can be found throughout the year but they are not necessarily resident.

 Normal breeding area

 Species present
throughout the year

 Wintering area

Great Crested Grebe *Podiceps cristatus*
Family: Podicipitidae   480 mm

The Great Crested Grebe is the largest Grebe, easily identified when adult by its black horned crest. In breeding plumage it has a conspicuous chestnut and black 'ruff' each side of the head. In winter the ruff disappears and the crest is less obvious. The face is white and the neck a pale grey. It has grey-brown upper parts and is white below. The bill and eye are a pinkish red and the legs greenish.

Juveniles have black-and-white striped upper parts and lack the crest and ruff.

It has a weak flight with trailing legs and with the head and neck held out straight but lower than the body level. It is distinguished from the slightly smaller Red-necked Grebe (*Podiceps grisegena*) by its thinner neck and pinkish-red bill.

Its calls include trumpeting, barking and vibrating notes.

It usually breeds on inland waters with plenty of aquatic vegetation but in winter it frequents all types of open water – especially reservoirs and estuaries.

The nest is usually a floating heap of waterlogged vegetation. The three or four eggs are white at first, becoming stained with brown as incubation proceeds.

Grey Heron *Ardea cinerea*
Family: Ardeidae   920 mm

The largest of the European herons is distinguished by its grey upper parts, white head and neck, with a broad black streak from above the eye through to a long crest. Adults have yellowish bills and brown legs. Juveniles have dark brown bills.

Long legs and neck and a long dagger-like bill enable the bird to live and feed beside water. The right-hand picture shows a Heron standing motionless in shallow water, poised ready to catch the unsuspecting fish.

The distinctive flight is with slow but strong flapping beats of the broad rounded wings, with trailing legs and head drawn back between the shoulders.

Its call is a harsh 'fraaank', but in the breeding season its repertoire is extended to various croaking sounds, and at the nest both young and old birds indulge in bill clattering. The nesting heronry is ancestral and used from year to year. It is normally in tall trees near water.

Nests are usually large unsightly flat-topped platforms of sticks. From three to seven very pale blue/green eggs are laid.

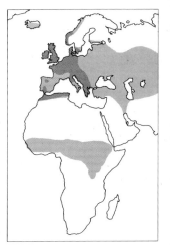

Shelduck *Tadorna tadorna*
Family: Anatidae   610 mm

A partial migrant over much of Europe, the Shelduck is found mainly on muddy coasts and estuaries but also breeding on heaths and farmland close to the sea. It is regularly seen in small family parties but very seldom with other ducks. Most adults migrate to Heligoland Bight in July where they moult into their eclipse plumage.

From a distance it appears as a small black and white goose but it is distinguished by its dark green head and neck and white body with a broad chestnut band across the breast. The primaries and scapulars are blackish and the speculum green. The legs are flesh coloured and the bill red. The male's bill has a prominent knob as seen on the bird on the right of the picture. Juveniles and birds in eclipse plumage are browner, with juveniles having all white underparts and cheeks, pink bill and grey legs. Ducklings are black and white – most unusual amongst ducks.

Its calls are a short 'ak-ak-ak' and a louder 'ark-ark', but they are not often heard outside the breeding season.

The nest is usually in a hole or tunnel amongst brambles or rabbit holes in sand-dunes or heathland close to the sea. One clutch of from three to seventeen creamy-white eggs is laid.

Mallard *Anas platyrhynchos*
Family: Anatidae   580 mm

The Mallard is found in almost any situation near fresh water and in winter on sea coasts and estuaries. It is a partial migrant, some birds from Scandinavia wintering in central Europe.

The male on the right of the picture is in breeding plumage. A glossy green head, white collar, dark brown breast, purple speculum and grey back distinguish it from other European ducks although the speculum is not visible in the picture. Females and juveniles are a mottled brown being similar to other species apart from their larger size and purple-blue speculum. Late in summer the males moult into an intermediate plumage – called eclipse – when they resemble rather darker forms of the female. The male's bill is yellow with a darker tip, but the female's and juvenile's vary from green to orange or reddish. Legs are orange.

Mallards usually live in pairs or small flocks and quite often with other surface-feeding ducks.

The call is a loud quacking, but whilst breeding, the male has a quiet whistling call. The nest is usually a hollow often amongst thick cover some distance from water but they sometimes nest in holes in trees. From nine to twelve greenish-buff eggs are laid.

21

Pintail *Anas acuta*

Family: Anatidae   560 mm

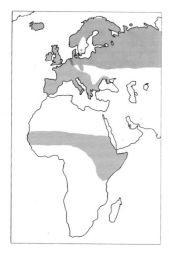

The Pintail is a surface-feeding duck easily identified by its long pointed tail and long neck. The male has a brown head and a conspicuous white streak running up each side of the neck from the breast. The upper parts and flanks are mainly grey and undertail coverts are black. The female, juvenile and male in eclipse plumage are brown with darker streaks and are distinguished from otherwise similar brown ducks by the slim shape, blue-grey bill and greyish legs.

It is relatively quiet, the male having only a low-pitched whistle and the female a quiet quack.

Although they are found throughout Europe their distribution varies in the southern part of the range. It is a partial migrant, many birds moving from north-eastern Europe to the south and west to winter mainly in coastal areas. It is then gregarious, often with other surface-feeding ducks, particularly Wigeon (*Anas penelope*).

The nest is a hollow lined with feathers amongst short grass, marram or heather and often on open ground.

A single clutch of from six to twelve eggs is laid. They are from yellowish cream to pale blue.

Tufted Duck *Aythya fuligula*

Family: Anatidae   430 mm

The Tufted Duck is a partial migrant well distributed throughout northern Europe apart from southern Norway and moving south and west to winter as nesting waters freeze over. It is a diving duck frequenting all kinds of inland water but is seldom seen on the sea.

Males are mainly black with white belly, flanks and wing bar. They have a drooping black crest, yellow eye and greyish-blue legs and bill. Females, juveniles and males in eclipse plumage are mainly brown with pale belly and white wing bar. Females have a rather obscure crest and often a pale whitish patch on the face at the base of the bill.

They are highly gregarious, mixing with Coot (*Fulica atra*) and other ducks. The female's call is a growling 'kurr' resembling the Pochard (*Aythya ferina*), and in the breeding season the male makes a soft whistling note.

The nest is a feather-lined hollow near water where there is plenty of cover, and is usually in a tussock or under a bush. Sometimes old Coots' nests are used.

One clutch of from six to eighteen greenish-grey eggs is laid.

23

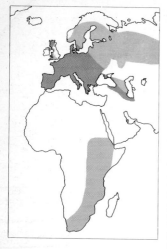

Buzzard *Buteo buteo*

Family: Accipitridae

500–550 mm

The Buzzard is distributed throughout Europe apart from northern Scandinavia, Iceland and parts of eastern Britain. It is a partial migrant with northerly birds moving into southern Europe for the winter. Populations to the far east of Europe winter in South and East Africa.

The plumage is mainly brown with paler underparts. Adults are very variable and some have dark brown underparts with patches of whitish brown. The hooked bill is brownish grey with a yellow cere and the legs are yellow. The cere of the juvenile is greenish.

In flight the silhouette is distinctive. It has broad, rounded wings, a short neck and rounded tail. As it has variable body plumage, the tail is perhaps the best identification character. It is narrowly barred brown and grey with a single dark bar at the tip. Similar species which can be confused are the Rough-legged Buzzard (*Buteo lagopus*) which has a whitish tail with a single dark bar at the tip and Honey Buzzard (*Pernis apivorus*) which has a narrow tail with several broader bars. The legs are unfeathered, unlike the Rough-legged Buzzard.

The flight is laboured and occasionally it hovers, but it soars for long periods. The straight wings are held motionless with the tips of the primaries curved upwards and tail spread out.

Its diet consists mainly of small animals and insects but it frequently takes carrion.

Although not really gregarious they sometimes gather in small numbers when soaring in certain places.

The call is a loud, drawn-out mewing 'pee-oo' and it occasionally makes croaking noises.

Its main habitats are hilly and mountainous areas with wooded valleys, secluded rocky coasts, sea cliffs, moorland, farmland and forest with substantial clearings.

The nest is built in a tree or on a cliff ledge and occasionally on the ground. Various materials are used depending on the situation. When in trees a large flattish platform of sticks and local vegetation is used but in marine situations dry seaweed is often the main material.

Two to three eggs are laid. They are normally a dull white with blotches of red-brown and pale lilac. Usually they are single-brooded.

Buzzard soaring

Kestrel *Falco tinnunculus*
Family: Falconidae 350 mm

Probably the most common bird of prey in Europe, it is found in all situations from the centre of large cities to the wildest moorland. It has adapted to living in built-up areas and is now not an uncommon suburban bird. Another favourite haunt is alongside motorways and railway embankments.

The Kestrel is easily recognised by its constant hovering although it must not be confused with the Merlin (*Falco columbarius*) or other birds which occasionally hover. The silhouettes show a typical hovering position and the pointed wings and long tail which are evident when flying direct. The wingbeats are normally quite fast, but it does occasionally glide. Quite often it perches in prominent places such as posts, dead trees, telegraph poles or rocks.

The male bird has a blue-grey head, rump and tail, the tail having a broad black band near the white tip. The upper parts are spotted chestnut and the underparts are buff-brown with scattered black streaks.

The female has rufous-brown upper parts with darker barring and a brownish tail with several darker bars. Juveniles are very similar in colour to the female.

The Kestrel has yellow legs, cere and skin around the eye. Its hooked bill is a bluish-horn colour.

The main food items are mice, voles, beetles and other insects with the occasional small bird, but in towns the House Sparrow (*Passer domesticus*) often forms a major part of the diet. From a hovering position or from a perch the Kestrel 'stoops' to catch its prey; then the food is often carried away in its talons, particularly when disturbed.

It normally calls only during the breeding season, when a loud shrill 'kee, kee, kee' can often be heard. Other calls are a musical 'kee-kee' and occasionally a spitting 'kik-kik-kik'.

The nest is situated in old trees, on ledges of buildings or cliffs and in recent years they have been found high on electricity pylons. Often the old nests of crows and magpies are utilised. Very little, if any, nesting material is used. The eggs, numbering up to six, are usually reddish buff heavily blotched with brown.

Since many hollow hedgerow trees have been lost through land reclamation and modern farming techniques, suitable nesting sites have become fewer. Nest-boxes have been tried in Switzerland and Holland and have proved a very successful substitute. Their use in other places is very much to be encouraged.

Hovering

Direct flight

Cere

26

Partridge *Perdix perdix*
Family: Phasianidae

300 mm

The Partridge is resident over much of Europe but absent from Iceland, parts of Scandinavia, and most of Iberia.

Its plumage is mainly brown with dark and light streaks. It has a rufous-coloured face and grey neck and breast. Males have a conspicuous black horseshoe-shaped patch on the belly. Although females have a similar mark it is often less obvious. Juveniles have a 'streaky' appearance with no distinctive markings.

The bill is greenish grey and the legs grey. The tail is short and the wings short and rounded. The flight is fast with intermittent periods of gliding on down-curved wings.

It normally walks with a crouched posture as shown in the picture but when alarmed it either runs away with head held upright or squats on the ground.

The call is a repeated rasping 'krrr-it, krrr-it' and sometimes a keev'.

It frequents light agricultural land with plenty of cover and heaths, pastures and sand-dunes.

The nest is a scrape lined with grasses and feathers. From ten to twenty olive-brown eggs are laid.

Water Rail *Rallus aquaticus*
Family: Rallidae   280 mm

The Water Rail is widespread in Europe apart from northern Scandinavia.

It is most difficult to observe, due to its skulking behaviour, and is usually seen 'making off' into the dense cover of a reed-bed, swamp or fen. It is similar in shape to a brown Moorhen (*Gallinula chloropus*) but has a long red bill, conspicuous flanks barred black and white and white undertail coverts. The face, throat and breast are grey, the legs flesh-brown and eye red. Juveniles have mottled underparts.

It is more often heard than seen, its distinctive call being a series of sounds starting with grunting and continuing to a squeal. Other calls are 'cep . . . cep . . . cep' or a 'kik, kik, kik'. It frequently calls during the night.

The flight is weak with legs dangling. On the ground it walks or runs.

The nest is a small flat platform of reeds and other aquatic debris constructed amongst the thick cover of reeds, sedge or grasses.

From six to eleven creamy-white eggs faintly mottled with dark red and grey-blue are laid. They are normally double-brooded.

Moorhen *Gallinula chloropus*
Family: Rallidae 330 mm

The Moorhen is fairly common in Europe apart from northern Scandinavia. It can be found in almost any location near fresh water from large lakes and rivers to the farmer's duckpond.

It is a stout blackish-brown bird with conspicuous white under-tail coverts and red frontal-shield and bill with a yellow tip. There is a white line along the flank, and the legs are greenish with a red band at the top where the feathering starts. The eye is red. Juveniles are a dark greyish brown with very pale throat and belly and can be distinguished from juvenile Coots (*Fulica atra*) by the white undertail coverts.

Both on land and water it frequently flicks its tail. When disturbed it runs for cover, or if swimming it either dives or takes flight with apparent difficulty after 'running' some distance along the surface. The weak flight is usually low with legs dangling.

The harsh call is usually a 'kittic' or a croaking 'kurruk'. The shallow nest is built from dead leaves amongst aquatic plants in or near shallow water. From five to eleven buffish eggs spotted red-brown are laid. Up to three broods are attempted.

Coot *Fulica atra*
Family: Rallidae   380 mm

The only all-black water-bird with a conspicuous white 'frontal-shield' and bill, the Coot is larger than the Moorhen (*Gallinula chloropus*) and lacks the white markings on the flanks and tail. It has a red eye and heavy, greenish legs and feet.

Juveniles are rather featureless with very dark grey upper parts, pale underparts and whitish throat. The 'downy' young have a reddish-orange head and neck.

The flight is laboured, with the legs trailing and when taking-off from water it 'runs' along the surface for some distance before becoming airborne. When swimming, it frequently dives for food or to hide from predators.

During the winter it becomes gregarious, often collecting in large flocks and associating with ducks.

It is usually found on large expanses of water and frequently on estuaries in winter.

The nest is usually a fixed platform of thick aquatic vegetation lined with water weeds. The four to eight eggs are pale brown speckled with small dark brown spots. As many as three broods are attempted each year.

The usual calls are a loud 'kewk' and a spitting 'skik'.

31

Oystercatcher *Haematopus ostralegus*

Family: Haematopodidae   430 mm

The Oystercatcher is mainly a shore-bird but is still spreading widely inland to breed in northern England and Scotland and south-western Sweden. Out of the breeding season it is seldom seen inland and is mainly confined to rocky, sandy, or muddy estuaries or coastline. It is a partial migrant, with most European birds moving south and west for the winter.

It is easily identified by being the only large wading bird with a black head and back with white underparts and rump and having a long orange bill and pink legs. The black and white tail and broad white wing bar are very obvious in flight.

The lower right-hand picture shows the head of an adult bird with its bright orange bill, a red eye and a completely black throat. Adults often have a faint white throat band for a short period in the autumn.

The year-old bird in the lower left-hand picture shows a typical brownish bill and red-brown eye. The white band across the throat is absent for the first two or three months of its life and develops in its first winter. They have pale pinkish-blue legs. Two-year-old birds also have a white throat band but it is generally less obvious. At the age of four, many start breeding for the first time and then during the breeding season the throat is all black.

Non-breeding birds and others out of the breeding season are highly gregarious, often flocking to roost with other wading birds. The flocks are very noisy with their loud 'kleep, kleep' calls. When alarmed they call a shrill 'pic, pic, pic'. The display song is a series of long piping notes starting slowly and increasing in volume and tempo.

They walk or run on the ground and frequently wade in water in search of marine invertebrates such as cockles, mussels, limpets and worms on which they feed. The flight is strong and direct.

The breeding habitat is very varied, from rocky shingle and sandy shorelines, saltings, sand dunes and small islands to inland on arable crops, riverbanks, etc. In some places Oystercatchers have been known to nest in coastal gardens and beside roadways.

The nest is usually a large scrape with a sparse lining of pebbles, shells or seaweed. It is frequently located on a shingle area amongst a patch of vegetation. In some localities, such as small islands, several pairs may nest close together but otherwise they are usually solitary.

One clutch of three or four roundish eggs is laid. They are usually a pale buff with spots, blotches and streaks of dark brown and black. The young leave the nest within two days of hatching and fledge in about five weeks.

Oystercatcher in flight

Ringed Plover *Charadrius hiaticula*
Family: Charadriidae   190 mm

The Ringed Plover is found mainly on sandy and shingle shores but occurs at inland waters particularly during migration. Migration takes place from northern and eastern Europe to western Europe and into central and southern Africa.

It behaves like a typical plover, running a short distance, pausing to stoop for food and occasionally bobbing its head. It is easily distinguished from other small waders by its short bill, orange-yellow legs and prominent black-and-white head patterning and, when in flight, by the prominent white wing bar, which is missing in the otherwise similar Little Ringed Plover (*Charadrius dubius*). The upper parts are brown and underparts white. The breast has a prominent black band across it and another black mark passes through the eye. Juveniles are paler.

When disturbed it calls 'queep' or 'too-li'. The song uttered in display flight is a repeated 'quita-weeoo'.

Non-breeding birds are highly gregarious, often associating with other small waders to roost.

The three to four buff-brown eggs mottled blackish brown are laid in a scrape in sand or shingle occasionally lined with small pebbles or broken shells.

Grey Plover *Pluvialis squatarola*
Family: Charadriidae   280 mm

The Grey Plover breeds in arctic tundra and the birds we see in Europe are either migrating birds on passage to their wintering grounds in Africa, non-breeding birds summering with us or winter visitors from further north.

They prefer sandy beaches at the shore-line, coastal mudflats and estuaries, but they occasionally occur inland on passage.

Although gregarious, the Grey Plover is generally found in small parties, or amongst flocks of other waders. It is very timid and moves off at the slightest disturbance.

In summer, adults have mottled pale grey and black upper parts with black face, throat and belly but in winter they lose the black markings and become almost white below. Juveniles are more brownish and are distinguished from the Golden Plover (*Pluvialis apricaria*) by being more robust and having larger eyes and heavier bill. The sexes are alike.

In flight, the black axillaries show like black 'arm-pits' against the pale grey under surface of the wings. The rump shows white against a faintly barred tail and a whitish wing bar is apparent. The plaintive call note, a whistling 'tsee-oo-ee', is less musical than that of the Golden Plover.

Lapwing *Vanellus vanellus*
Family: Charadriidae   300 mm

The Lapwing can be found throughout the year on farmland, but it also frequents coastal mudflats, estuaries and the shores of freshwater lakes and reservoirs during winter and also on marsh and moorland when breeding. It is a long-range migrant, well distributed throughout central Europe but generally absent from northern Scandinavia and much of Iberia and Italy. Most populations migrate south and west for the winter.

The plumage is iridescent green-black above, and on the crown and upper breast. It has white cheeks and breast and pale chestnut undertail coverts. It can be distinguished by its long upturned crest, longish pale-brown coloured legs and, in flight, by its slow flapping rounded wings. In spring it has a spectacular aerobatic display flight accompanied by its call, 'pee-wit', and a song, 'pee-wit-pweet, pweet, pee-wit'.

In winter it becomes highly gregarious, especially on ploughed or stubble fields. The nest is usually an unconcealed scrape or platform of grasses, often situated without any protective vegetation. The three or four eggs are pear-shaped and vary from buff to dark brown with a bluish or greenish tinge and blotched with dark brown and black.

Turnstone *Arenaria interpres*

Family: Charadriidae   230 mm

The birds occurring in western Europe are mainly from Scandinavian and Greenland breeding populations. A high proportion of the Scandinavian birds winter along the Atlantic coast of West Africa and Iberia but Greenland birds winter mainly along the coasts of north-west Europe.

The picture shows the Turnstone's well-camouflaged 'tortoiseshell' plumage against a pebbly beach. It lives in this type of habitat and also on rocky coasts when wintering in Europe. It is identified as a stout shore-bird with a pointed black bill and short orange legs. In winter the upper parts are a dark mottled brown and underparts mainly white with a brown breast-band. In summer, the upper parts are chestnut-brown streaked with black, the underparts are white with a dark brown breast-band, and the head is white with black markings. In flight it has a distinct pied appearance unlike any other small wader.

On the ground it runs or walks about, occasionally lifting stones (hence its name) and seaweed with its bill in search of the marine invertebrates on which it lives.

Its main calls are 'tic-a-tic' and a long trill.

37

Dunlin *Calidris alpina*

Family: Scolopacidae 180 mm

Three subspecies of Dunlin occur in Europe. The nominate race *C. a. alpina* breeds in the northern part of Scandinavia, European Russia and western Siberia. Many of these birds migrate through the southern Baltic region to winter on the coasts of Britain, France and Iberia with some moving as far south as north-west Africa. The race *C. a. schinzii* has its breeding areas in northern Britain, Iceland and southern Scandinavia and migrates southward along the coasts of Britain and western Europe to winter on the coasts of West Africa. The north-eastern-Greenland race (*C. a. arctica*) follows a similar migration route but in much lower numbers.

The three races are very similar and difficult to separate in the field except in spring. Summer plumage has warm-brown crown and upper parts streaked or speckled with darker brown and black. The breast is mainly white with a conspicuous black patch on the lower belly. The bill is blackish and slightly decurved at the tip. The legs are dark olive-brown. The winter plumage is more sombre with flecked grey-brown upper parts, a white belly and greyish breast. Juveniles are very similar but have buffish tips to the wing coverts.

In flight it shows a white wing bar and white sides to the rump and tail. The flight is very fast and direct and when in a flock all birds appear to turn and manœuvre simultaneously. Out of the breeding season they are highly gregarious, gathering in huge flocks, often with other waders, to roost.

On the ground they walk or run. Their flight call is a short high-pitched 'tree' and when in a flock they have a feeble twitter. The song, a low-pitched trill, is performed in flight or sometimes on the ground with the wings raised upwards.

The preferred winter habitat is sea-shores and muddy estuaries, but they are often seen near inland waters; marshes and sewage-farms on migration. Breeding is generally near water, from tundra, wet grass moors and bogs to coastal marshes.

The well-hidden nest is typically a scrape in a tussock of vegetation lined with grasses or leaves. A single clutch of three or four eggs is laid. The colour varies from pale green to buff heavily spotted or streaked in shades of brown and grey at the thick end.

Dunlin in flight – note the white wing bar and white sides of the rump and tail

Knot *Calidris canutus*

Family: Scolopacidae

250 mm

The Knot shown in the picture is an adult in its winter plumage. It has typically uniform pale-grey upper parts and white underparts. Juveniles have more 'scaly' pale-grey upper parts. In summer the upper parts are a chestnut-brown mottled with grey, the head and underparts are russet. For a wader it appears rather plump and has relatively short legs, bill and neck. The legs are olive-green and the bill black.

In flight it shows a uniform pale-grey rump and tail and a faint wing bar.

Its size is larger than the Sanderling (*Calidris alba*) and Dunlin (*Calidris alpina*) but smaller than Redshank (*Tringa totanus*) and Grey Plover (*Pluvialis squatarola*). The Curlew Sandpiper (*Calidris ferruginea*) closely resembles the Knot when in breeding plumage but is distinguished by its smaller-sized body, longer legs and curved bill.

They are highly gregarious, often mixing with other shorebirds, and have a tendency to congregate in closely packed flocks, particularly when roosting.

In the flock they make a twittering sound which collectively is quite loud. They have a low-pitched whistling call, 'twit-wit', when in flight and sometimes a low-pitched 'nut'. The Knots we see in Europe are mainly from the breeding populations of Greenland and north-eastern Canada (Ellesmere Island) with smaller numbers from Siberia. The Greenland and Canadian birds migrate after breeding through Iceland to arrive on coasts and estuaries of the British Isles and North Sea coasts of Denmark, Germany and Holland where they carry out their moult. From there many move westwards to estuaries in the British Isles for the winter with others moving down into France and Iberia.

The Siberian population take a more easterly route on their migration to their main wintering grounds in Africa.

Its breeding habitat is in the barren lands of the high Arctic, but when it appears in Europe it is mainly confined to sandy and muddy estuaries and sea-shore and very occasionally at inland lakes and reservoirs.

Knot in flight – note the pale rump and wing bar

Sanderling *Calidris alba*

Family: Scolopacidae   205 mm

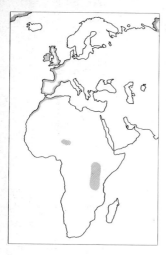

This extremely active little wader is most often seen on sandy beaches but occasionally inland, especially in spring, at reservoirs and lakes when on passage. It can be recognised in the winter as a plump, one of the palest, almost white little wader which runs backwards and forwards at high speed, with the waves in search of food. Then its head and underparts are white, the upper parts are pale grey, and it has a blackish shoulder patch.

In the summer plumage it retains its pure white belly but the upper parts, breast and head take on a speckled-chestnut appearance.

In flight it shows a prominent long white bar on a dark wing, distinguishing it from the Dunlin (*Calidris alpina*), whose wing bar is less conspicuous. It also has white sides to a dark tail. Juveniles have greyish-brown speckled upper parts and a pinkish-orange tinge to the head and breast. The bill and legs are black. Unlike most other waders, the Sanderling has only the three front toes on its feet as in the lower sketch. It is highly gregarious, mixing with other shore waders to feed and roost. In the flock they make a pleasant little twittering noise, and when flying a 'twick-twick' call is sometimes used.

The Sanderlings we see in Europe are either winter visitors or passage migrants. Their breeding grounds are in the Arctic tundra of Greenland and Siberia from which they migrate southward and westward, arriving on western European shores towards the end of August. Many of the early adult arrivals in the British Isles remain for only a few weeks whilst they build up fat reserves in order to continue their migration to their wintering grounds in West and South Africa. The adult birds remaining are probably a different population and some undergo their annual moult before moving off, in October, to wintering grounds further south in France, Iberia and Morocco. The return to the breeding grounds through Britain starts towards the end of April and takes place mainly in May. Some juvenile birds wintering in the south of the range do not move north to breed in their first year.

Sanderling in flight – note the obvious wing bar

Redshank *Tringa totanus*

Family: Scolopacidae

280 mm

The Redshank can easily be identified in flight as being the only medium-sized wader in Europe with a white rump and conspicuous white trailing edges to its dark wings. When on the ground, however, its plumage appears rather uniform but its long orange-red legs and reddish bill tipped black distinguish it from similar birds. It has brownish-grey upper parts with darker grey markings. The underparts are paler with light grey streaks.

Juveniles have orange-yellow legs and have more buff upper parts.

It is a bird of wetlands, breeding in all types of damp grassland such as marshes, saltings and pastures near rivers or lakes. In the winter it prefers mudflats, estuaries and saltmarsh, where it congregates often in large numbers with other waders.

The flight is rapid and direct, with fast irregular wingbeats. It runs or walks about on the ground and can often be seen perching on posts or tree stumps, particularly during the breeding season. It has a habit of bobbing its head up and down and, when disturbed, will fly off protesting with a barrage of piping notes and sometimes a scolding 'teuk, teuk, teuk'. Its most familiar call is a musical 'teu-tu-tu.' The song is a series of musical phrases based on the main call notes.

The preferred breeding habitat seems to be fairly dry marshland, meadows or saltings but sand-dunes and old sewage farms are often used.

A fairly prominent tuft of grass or marram with a hollowed-out scrape below is the usual type of nest site. Frequently it is near to nesting Lapwings (*Vanellus vanellus*), suggesting that they use one another as a primitive warning system. The usual clutch of eggs numbers four. They are buff, spotted and streaked with reddish brown. Sometimes the markings are concentrated at one end and occasionally they are very heavy blotches.

The Redshank is a partial migrant breeding in many locations throughout Europe, with the Scandinavian and eastern European populations moving south to winter on the Mediterranean coasts.

The Icelandic and British populations also migrate south and west for the winter, many juveniles reaching as far south as Iberia.

Redshank in flight – note the broad white patch on the trailing edge of the wing

Common Sandpiper *Tringa hypoleucos*
Family: Scolopacidae   200 mm

We see the Common Sandpiper more often near fresh water, although it occasionally frequents estuaries and sewage farms. It is mainly a summer visitor to Europe where it is quite common, particularly near streams in hilly districts. However, the population is sparse in Holland, Denmark and southern England and Ireland. It winters mainly in central and southern Africa.

The nesting scrape is made near fresh water on a river bank or exposed shingle ridge alongside a river. It is lined with grasses and local flood debris. The single clutch of four eggs are buff-brown with chestnut-brown spots and blotches.

They have a characteristic flickering flight over water, when they fly very low with bursts of fast and short wingbeats interspersed with occasional gliding with downward curved wings. A distinct white wing bar is visible.

Sexes are alike, having olive-brown upper parts and white underparts. Legs are a greenish grey and bill dark brown.

It is often seen around the edges and frequently wading in shallow pools. When on the ground it constantly bobs its head and tail. Its alarm call is a high-pitched 'twee-wee-wee'. The song is similar, but more elaborate and repeated rapidly.

Snipe *Gallinago gallinago*
Family: Scolopacidae

270 mm

The Snipe is very shy and prefers the damp habitat of inland marshland, bogs and sewage farms. When disturbed it rises quickly, with a harsh call, zigzagging from side to side before changing to a rapid direct flight. During its characteristic display flight the bird dives steeply with its outer-tail feathers spread wide to produce the vibrating sound known as 'drumming'. The song is a monotonous repeated 'chip-pa, chip-pa'.

The plumage above is a rufous brown with dark and light streaks. The underparts are whitish with faint stripes on the neck. The reddish-brown bill has a darker tip and the legs are greenish brown. The head has dark stripes running lengthways, distinguishing it from the Woodcock (*Scolopax rusticola*). It is also smaller and has a thinner bill. Compared with the Great Snipe (*Gallinago media*) it has less white in the tail. The Jack Snipe (*Lymnocryptes minima*) is smaller with no white in the tail.

The nest is usually amongst a tussock in a marshy area. The four eggs are pale brown blotched with dark brown and grey but colours vary considerably. The downy young are chequered black and buff on a chestnut ground. They hatch with legs nearly as long as the adult but the bill is only about 15 mm long.

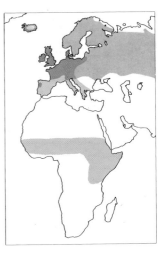

47

Black-headed Gull *Larus ridibundus*
Family: Laridae   380 mm

The Black-headed Gull is a partial migrant wintering in southern and western Europe. It inhabits estuaries, lakes and farmland and frequents rubbish dumps particularly in the winter. It is highly gregarious, even breeding in colonies.

Apart from the much smaller Little Gull (*Larus minutus*) it is the only gull with slender red bill and legs. Adults are mainly white with a pale grey mantle and wings. In flight the leading edge of the wing shows as a white streak and the tip is black. In summer the head is chocolate-brown but in winter it becomes white with dark spots behind and in front of the eye.

Juveniles have brown upper parts with darker mottling and a black tip to the white tail. The bill is orange tipped with black and the legs dark yellowish.

Its main calls are a harsh 'kwarr' and a short 'kwup'. The nest is built near moorland pools, on sand-dunes, saltings, and around inland lakes and gravel-pits. It is normally amongst tussocky vegetation and is generally a structure of dead grasses and plants.

Two or three greenish-brown eggs blotched with brown and grey are laid.

Herring Gull *Larus argentatus*

Family: Laridae   550 mm

The Herring Gull is the commonest gull around the coasts of Europe. It is a partial migrant with northerly birds moving to unfrozen waters in the winter.

In some places it has started nesting inland but generally it colonises sea cliffs, rocky islands and beaches. It has recently taken to nesting on buildings. The nest is usually a collection of grasses, seaweed and litter. The two to three eggs are from pale blue to dark brown with streaks and spots of dark brown.

Adults are white with grey upper parts and wings. The wings have black tips with white spots. Its heavy yellow bill has a red spot near the tip. The legs are pink except in the eastern Scandinavian race (*L. a. omissus*) and Mediterranean race (*L. a. michahellis*) which have yellow legs.

Juveniles are mainly brown with a dark tip to the tail and dark brown bill. Up to the third year when the birds become fully adult, they have intermediate plumages which show more grey and white in successive years.

Amongst the many calls are mewing and chuckling but the main calls are a 'kyow' and in spring a penetrating 'gah, gah, gah'. Its flight is strong with frequent gliding.

49

Common Tern *Sterna hirundo*
Family: Laridae

350 mm

The Common Tern is a summer visitor which roams the Atlantic Ocean in the winter.

It is like a small gull but is more slender, has long wings and a forked tail. It is mainly white, with a grey back and darker wing tips, and with black crown and nape. In summer the underparts are tinged grey-mauve, the legs are red and the bill is orange-red with a dark tip. In winter the shoulders are blackish, the forehead is white and the upper parts mottled brown. The legs become brownish red and the bill blackish, often with a reddish base.

It is similar to Arctic (*Sterna paradisea*) and Roseate Terns (*Sterna dougallii*) apart from slight variations in bill and leg colouring.

Juveniles are similar to winter adults but they have orange legs.

The main calls are a chattering 'kik-kik-kik . . .' and 'keeri, keeri'. In alarm it calls – 'keee-yah'.

It is highly gregarious, breeding in colonies on beaches, dunes and islands (often on inland waters).

The nest scrape is sparsely lined with local vegetation. Two to four pale brown or green eggs spotted and blotched with dark brown are laid.

Wood Pigeon *Columba palumbus*
Family: Columbidae   400 mm

The Wood Pigeon is a partial migrant with northerly and easterly populations wintering in southern and western Europe.

It is the largest of the pigeons, predominantly blue-grey with white patches at the sides of the neck and a conspicuous broad white band across the wing, noticed particularly in flight. The belly is paler and the breast a purplish brown. Adults have green and purple iridescent feathers on the neck which are absent from the juvenile. The legs are pink, the bill pinkish and the eye a pale yellow.

The song is the familiar 'cooo-coo-coo, coo-cu'.

Its flight is fast and direct. In spring it has a spectacular display flight, climbing at a steep angle often with noisy wing flaps and then gliding down.

In the winter it is highly gregarious. Its habitat is all sorts of wooded country and it frequently enters large towns. The shallow nest of twigs lined with grasses is usually in ivied or evergreen trees, but also in thick bushes and sometimes on the ground.

Two glossy white eggs are laid and normally two broods are attempted.

51

Stock Dove *Columba oenas*
Family: Columbidae   330 mm

The Stock Dove is well distributed throughout Europe except in northern Scandinavia and Italy. Birds in the south and west tend to be resident but others migrate southwards for the winter. At this time they become gregarious, joining flocks of Wood Pigeons (*Columba palumbus*).

It can be found in almost any situation but seems to favour woodland and open country where old trees are present.

The absence of white on the wings and neck and its smaller size distinguish it from the Wood Pigeon. It is very similar to the Rock Dove (*Columba livia*) but has black wing tips and no white rump. The plumage of both sexes is alike, the upper parts being blue-grey; the breast is buffish pink, getting paler towards the belly. Adults show a glossy green patch on the side of the neck.

The call is shorter and more monotonous than the Wood Pigeon's and sounds like 'cooo-coo-oo'.

Nesting occurs in hollows of trees, on cliffs, and infrequently on the ground. Two pure white eggs are laid in a nest lined sparsely with small twigs.

Collared Dove *Streptopelia decaocto*
Family: Columbidae   280 mm

The Collared Dove is a resident, having extended its range from the eastern Mediterranean to cover most of Europe in the last few years. It is now fairly common particularly near villages, suburban gardens and parkland where mature trees are present. In winter they are gregarious, moving about in flocks of up to fifty or more. Their favourite haunts include beech-woods.

It is distinguished from other doves by its drab uniform: grey-buff, grey-brown or pinky-buff upper parts, narrow black collar at the back of its neck, and grey-brown primaries. The underparts and head are paler with a pinkish tinge. The eyes are red.

The flight call is a 'kwirr' and the song a monotonous deep 'coo-cooo-coo'.

Nesting occurs from early March through to the end of October and as many as three or even four broods are attempted. Exceptionally, nests can be found in every month of the year. Each clutch consists of two glossy pure-white eggs. The nest is usually a flat platform constructed with the minimum of material in thick bushes or conifers. Plant stems are more often used for the basic structure but occasionally twigs are used. There is a layer of finer grasses for a lining.

53

Turtle Dove *Streptopelia turtur*
Family: Columbidae
280 mm

A fairly common summer visitor to most of Europe apart from Scandinavia, Scotland and Ireland. It frequents open woodland, large gardens, parks and heathland, particularly where there is undisturbed woodland and hedgerows. It often feeds on cultivated land, where it is usually seen in pairs or small groups, sometimes with other pigeons or doves.

Turtle Doves can be distinguished from other small pigeons by their slender shape, the pinkish-chestnut throat and breast and the distinctive white tip to the black tail. In flight this tip shows as a conspicuous white semicircular band, much narrower than that of the Collared Dove (*Streptopelia decaocto*) which is nearly half the tail length. The upper parts are pale chestnut with black centres to the feathers. Chin and throat are a pale grey. Adult birds have a black and white patch on the side of the neck. There is a yellow circle of skin around the eye. The legs are pink and the bill slate-grey.

Juveniles appear more brown generally and lack the patches in the neck. The two sexes have similar plumage. The flight is similar to that of the Wood Pigeon (*Columba palumbus*), being direct but more rapid. The wing movement is more erratic, with a jerky action as the wing is extended and retracted. In display the bird makes several flaps upwards at a steep angle then glides down for a short distance with its tail widespread and wings held high.

The quiet call sounds more peaceful than the other pigeons; it is a drawn-out and repeated 'roorrr'.

The nest is a flat-topped platform of twigs and small dead sticks lined with fine roots and grasses constructed low down in the fork of a tree or bush. Usually it is between one and five metres from the ground. The clutch of two glossy white eggs is incubated by both parents for a little over two weeks. The young birds are at first fed with regurgitated juices, called 'pigeon's milk', from the adult's crop, but later this is replaced by more solid matter in the form of semi-digested seeds.

Turtle Doves are double-brooded, the first nest being started in early June and the second later in July.

Turtle Dove taking-off – note the rounded white-tipped tail

Barn Owl *Tyto alba*

Family: Tytonidae   340 mm

Barn Owls are mainly resident over most of central and southern Europe but they are vagrants only to most of Scandinavia. Their numbers have decreased generally over the last twenty or so years, probably for several different reasons such as loss of suitable habitat and nesting sites, or because of the use of toxic chemicals in agriculture. They are attracted to human habitation, particularly derelict buildings on farms or near villages. Church towers, holes in old trees, and cliffs and the roof space in old buildings are favourite nesting sites. They can be encouraged to use a nest-box similar to the sketch below if it is erected in a suitable site such as a Dutch barn. Very little nest material is used and generally only a scrape is made amongst local debris. Often two clutches of from four to seven dull white eggs are laid.

The Barn Owl is easily identified as it is the only bird in Europe with speckled golden-buff upper parts. In the British Isles the underparts are white finely speckled with brown. Over much of Europe there is a dark-breasted race which has buffish underparts with the upper parts blue-grey. Other distinguishing points are the white facial mask, long legs covered with white feathers, and rounded wings. It has black eyes.

Although nocturnal, it sometimes hunts by day, especially in winter, seeking out small rodents which form the major part of its diet. At dusk we occasionally see it hunting near the roadside when its ghostly white form is picked out by the car headlights. Its call, a drawn-out screech, is normally only made at night. It also makes other hissing and snorting noises.

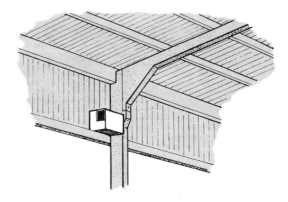

Bones of small mammals found in the pellets of undigested matter regurgitated by the Barn Owl

56

Little Owl *Athene noctua*

Family: Strigidae

220 mm

The Little Owl is well distributed throughout central and southern Europe but is absent from most of Scandinavia, Iceland and Scotland. Introduced into England at the turn of the last century, it has since become quite widespread. It is mainly resident over the whole of its range.

It lives in open country, especially farmland with scattered old trees and old buildings. Also on moorland fringes, sand-dunes, sandpits and quarries.

No nest is constructed but a scrape is utilised. Sites in old trees are regularly used but also in old buildings, haystacks, rabbit holes and old nests of other hole-nesting birds. One clutch of from two to seven smooth nearly spherical white eggs are laid each year. Once established, a nest site is often used year after year.

It feeds mainly on insects and small rodents, but very occasionally on small birds.

Little Owls regularly fly about by day as well as night and can often be seen perched on fence posts or telegraph poles. When approached they show signs of nervousness by bobbing up and down and waggling their heads. The flight is exceptionally undulating and fairly low and it occasionally hovers.

The calls are a loud 'kiu, kiu' and a quick rasping 'werru'. Juveniles make a wheezing sound and young birds in the nest occasionally hiss.

It can be distinguished by its small size and short flat head. Upper parts are a greyish brown, mottled and barred with white and the underparts are paler with broad brown streaks. The bill is a greenish yellow, the eye yellow, and the legs and feet are covered with pale buff feathers.

The picture shows a juvenile bird which had just been bathing in a puddle. Remnants of its downy plumage can still be seen on the top of its head.

Tawny Owl *Strix aluco*

Family: Strigidae

390 mm

The Tawny Owl is fairly common throughout Europe apart from northern Scandinavia, Ireland and the Isle of Man. It is a resident and remains in its breeding area throughout the year. As it is strictly nocturnal, it is seldom seen in flight during the day except when disturbed. Then its stout build distinguishes it from the Long-Eared Owl (*Asio otus*), and its shorter, rounded wings from the Barn Owl (*Tyto alba*), Long-Eared Owl and Short-Eared Owl (*Asio flammeus*).

The Tawny Owl's plumage varies considerably in colour, ranging from a rich tawny brown to grey. The greyer birds are found in northern areas, particularly Scotland. The upper parts are streaked with dark and light shades of brown, grey and buff, giving a mottled appearance. Underparts are a pale buffish brown heavily streaked with dark brown markings. The sexes are alike. It has black eyes set in a large round head with no ear tufts. The hooked bill is a pale greenish buff. Legs and feet are feathered.

It is generally found in mature woods and copses, but often frequents suburban parks and large gardens.

It can often be found roosting during the day if one investigates mobbing noises made by other small birds, particularly House Sparrows (*Passer domesticus*), Chaffinches (*Fringilla coelebs*) and Blackbirds (*Turdus merula*). The familiar hooting is generally heard at night as 'hoo-hoo-hoo', followed after a brief interval by a quavering 'oo-oo-oo-oo'. The call 'ke-wick' is heard mainly in the autumn.

The Tawny Owl's diet consists of small rodents in the main, supplemented by the occasional small bird, insect or amphibian. Nesting occurs as early as mid-February in mild winters. Normally a hollow tree is chosen as the site, although it has been known to use old nests of large birds, buildings and rabbit burrows. From two to five whitish glossy eggs are laid.

Modern farming methods have caused a decline in the number of hollow trees available as potential nesting sites, and nest-boxes have proved successful with this species. The sketch shows a typical example developed in England for studying Tawny Owl's nesting preferences. It is constructed of 20–25 mm thick timber with a perforated metal base 250 mm square. Its length should be about 750 mm.

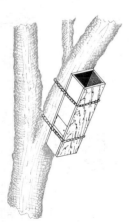

A nest-box suitable for Tawny Owls

Kingfisher *Alcedo atthis*

Family: Alcedinidae   165 mm

The Kingfisher is undoubtedly one of the most brilliantly coloured birds occurring throughout most of Europe. It is, however, absent from northern Scandinavia, northern Scotland and Iceland. It is a partial migrant, with birds from north-easterly populations moving south and west for the winter. The preferred habitat is along slow-flowing rivers, streams and canals but it can often be found by lakes and sand-pits at some distance from flowing water. During the winter it can occasionally be seen by the sea coasts and around estuaries and saltmarshes.

It is easy to identify as it is the only bird in Europe with brilliant blue-green upper parts and rich chestnut underparts. It has a white throat and neck patch and a chestnut patch just below the eye. The legs are bright red.

The long dagger-shaped bill varies in colour as can be seen from the two pictures. The bird in the inset picture has an all-black bill and is almost certainly an adult male. There is, however, some controversy over birds with a red lower mandible, as in the main picture, but they are thought to be females.

The Kingfisher lives on a diet of fish or marine invertebrates for which it dives into the water. Its body has adapted to suit these habits as can be seen from its sleek shape. The short body, tail and wings enable it to manœuvre under water and its large head and bill allow it to swallow small fish whole. Prior to diving for food it usually perches on some vantage point above the water and frequently bobs its head and tail. Sometimes it dives whilst in flight and occasionally it hovers. After catching a fish it takes it back to the perch holding it sideways in its bill and kills it by banging it on the perch. The fish is swallowed whole, head first.

Its flight is very fast and direct and usually quite low. The calls are a high-pitched 'chee' or 'chee-kee' often repeated rapidly several times. In the breeding season it also has a twittering call. The song is a short high-pitched trill.

Nesting usually takes place in a hole excavated in the sandy or earthen bank of a waterway and, fairly frequently now, in sand- and gravel-pits. The nest hole can be anything from a 0·5 m to 1·5 m long and rises into the bank opening out into a spherical nesting cavity. From five to seven glossy white roundish eggs are laid in a scrape lined with a few fish bones. Frequently two broods are attempted.

Wryneck *Jynx torquilla*

Family: Picidae   165 mm

The Wryneck is a summer visitor to most of Europe apart from northern Scandinavia, Iceland, southern Iberia and also, but more rarely, to all parts of the British Isles. It migrates to winter mainly in central Africa north of the Equator.

Its habitat is mainly deciduous woodland or common land with scattered trees but it seems to favour gardens and orchards particularly where old fruit trees are present.

From a distance its mottled plumage of greys, buffs and brown appears more as a uniform grey-brown, the underparts being paler than the upper parts. The bill and legs are brownish buff.

The Wryneck, although a member of the Woodpecker family, behaves quite differently in many ways. Its behaviour, movement and stance are more like a passerine but its feet, like those of the Woodpeckers, have two toes in front and two behind, an adaptation which allows it to cling to trees.

Its flight is undulating and its long, rounded tail becomes very obvious in flight.

The name Wryneck probably derives from the bird's ability to extend and rotate its neck in the most unusual contortions. This behaviour is usually adopted in defence particularly during the breeding season if it is disturbed on the nest. It then hisses, at the same time giving the appearance of a snake. It also has the ability to raise its crown feathers as a crest.

It usually feeds on the ground hopping around with its tail raised searching for insects. It is particularly fond of ants and their cocoons which it obtains by raking out ant-hills. During the autumn it also takes berries. Its presence is more often given away by its call – a clear but monotonous 'kyee-kyee-kyee-kyee-kyee'. From time to time it varies the loudness, giving the impression that it is moving about but generally it is stationary on some high perch.

The nest is a hole or cavity in a tree, post or even a wall and in places nest-boxes are regularly used. Often nests of other birds such as the Tree Sparrow (*Passer montanus*) and Lesser Spotted Woodpecker (*Dendrocopos minor*) are taken over after the occupants have been dislodged. Normally from seven to ten dull white eggs are laid in the bottom of the hole, no nesting material being added. Sometimes two broods are attempted.

Great Spotted Woodpecker
Dendrocopos major
Family: Picidae   230 mm

The Great Spotted Woodpecker is well distributed throughout most of Europe apart from Iceland and northern Scandinavia. It is mainly resident, but in some years it erupts and large flocks from the north arrive in central and southern Europe.

Its preferred habitat includes open woodland with mature deciduous trees, but it does live amongst the pinewoods in the north. It is seen in parks and gardens more than the other woodpeckers.

The male has a red nape and the juvenile a complete red crown. The female has a black crown. The underparts are uniform white. A black moustachial stripe continues in an unbroken line below the cheek through to the black neckband.

In Europe the Great Spotted Woodpecker is similar in many ways to other spotted woodpeckers. It is much larger than the Lesser Spotted Woodpecker (*Dendrocopos minor*) and has large white shoulder patches and red undertail coverts. The Middle Spotted Woodpecker (*Dendrocopos medius*) is slightly smaller and has a red crown, conspicuous white sides to the head and smaller white shoulder patches.

It is usually seen climbing about trees, seldom on the ground. The undulating flight is very characteristic, the wings being completely retracted once in each undulation.

The diet consists mainly of insects and larvae but in winter it consumes a few seeds and often visits bird-tables for kitchen scraps and suet. It can be attracted by hanging up a piece of backbone, with meat remains attached, obtained from the butcher. In the process of searching for food, holes are often excavated in dead wood by hammering with the sharp bill to expose what is underneath. The very rapid drumming heard is a contact sound and is the result of hammering the bill on a resonant dead branch. The calls are a harsh churring sound and a lound 'tchick'. The nest hole is excavated in a dead tree or sometimes a natural tree cavity is enlarged and the eggs are laid on a base of wood chippings.

Four to seven glossy translucent white eggs are incubated for about fifteen days.

The Great Spotted Woodpecker is the only serious avian predator of nest-boxes. The entrance hole is either enlarged or a fresh hole is drilled into the side of the box to get at the eggs or young. They do, however, use larger nest-boxes on occasions for their own nest. The sketch shows a suitable nest-box which would accommodate the Great Spotted Woodpecker.

50 mm dia. hole

500 mm

20 mm

200 mm   200 mm

A nest-box suitable for Great Spotted Woodpeckers

Lesser Spotted Woodpecker
Dendrocopos minor
Family: Picidae   150 mm

The Lesser Spotted Woodpecker is widely distributed in Europe apart from Denmark, Scotland, northern England and Iceland. It is by no means abundant anywhere. A few northerly birds move into central Europe for the winter but the birds are mainly residents.

Its habitat is broadleaved and mixed open woodland and it sometimes lives in old decaying parkland and orchards. Most of its time seems to be spent amongst the topmost twigs of trees searching for food, but it is often seen lower down, particularly in orchards. Its diet is mainly insectivorous but in the winter it supplements this with seeds.

It is the smallest of the European woodpeckers, being only the size of a sparrow. Its black and white plumage distinguish it from all other habitually tree-climbing species of its size. The upper parts are heavily barred black and white. The underparts are whitish tinged with brown and the forehead and cheeks are white. The bill is greyish and legs a greyish green.

Females have a whitish crown, whereas males have red and juveniles partially red. Juveniles, however, can be distinguished by having browner underparts.

The flight is weak and undulating and on the ground it hops. It drums on dead trees but makes less noise than the Great Spotted Woodpecker (*Dendrocopos major*). Its main call is a weak high-pitched 'pee-pee-pee-pee-pee' very similar to that of the Wryneck (*Jynx torquilla*). Although seldom heard it has another call, a weak 'tchick', which resembles the Great Spotted Woodpecker's call.

The nest site is a hole in the dead wood of an old tree. Usually a hole about 40 mm in diameter is bored in the trunk or into the underside of a sloping branch and a shaft is excavated up to about 250 mm deep.

The four to six translucent glossy white eggs are laid on wood chippings which frequently cover the eggs.

Occasionally the same cavity is used in successive years. Normally only one brood is attempted each year.

Sky Lark *Alauda arvensis*
Family: Alaudidae

180 mm

Found throughout almost all of Europe apart from northern Scandinavia and Iceland, the Skylark is a partial migrant with many north-eastern breeding birds moving into southern Europe for the winter.

Arriving back on its breeding grounds early in March, it starts to claim its territory in its distinctive song-flight. Rising almost vertically into the air until nearly out of sight, it hovers almost motionless whilst performing a long and sustained song – a high-pitched trilling and warbling. On the descent it continues to sing until just before alighting. Sometimes it sings on the ground and occasionally from a low perch.

The call note, often given in flight, is a clear, liquid 'chirrup'.

It prefers a habitat of open treeless country, from moorland and rough pasture to farmland, saltmarshes and sand-dunes. It is frequently found around airfields and in the winter on arable land.

The main colour of its plumage is very similar to other larks. It has brown upper parts streaked with blackish brown and buffish-brown underparts with bold brown streaks. The bill is horn coloured and the legs a pale brown.

Its distinguishing marks are the fairly long tail with white outer feathers, long pointed wings which show pale trailing edges in flight and a suggestion of a crest. In display the crest is raised and very obvious. Compared with the Wood Lark (*Lullula arborea*) it is somewhat larger and has a much longer tail. The Crested Lark (*Galerida cristata*) although about the same size is much paler and of more solid build and has a very prominent crest. The flight is strong with slight undulations and on the ground it walks.

The diet is mainly weed seeds which are picked from the ground, but during the summer they take more insect food, particularly when they are feeding young.

The open, cup-shaped nest is usually on the ground amongst grasses, as in the lower picture, or in the side of a tussock. Late nesting birds choosing sites in farmland often have their nests completely hidden by the crop by the time the young birds fledge. The construction is of grasses lined with finer grasses and a little hair.

Usually three to five eggs are laid. They are coloured a dirty white and are covered with grey-brown spots and speckles.

Two broods are normal and often a third is attempted. After breeding they become highly gregarious, forming up in small groups, particularly during migration and when the hard weather arrives.

Sand Martin *Riparia riparia*

Family: Hirundinidae   120 mm

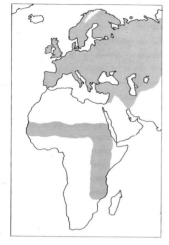

In common with other swallows, the Sand Martin is a migrant, breeding in Europe and travelling down to Africa south of the Sahara for the winter.

There is a strong tendency for individual birds to return to the same nesting colony, and even the same hole, year after year. The lower picture shows part of a colony in a sand-pit, but any vertical cliff face such as a river bank or railway cutting may be used, particularly near water. Holes are excavated anything up to a metre long and a small chamber is opened out at the end. A small amount of feathers and airborne plant down is collected to form a base for the eggs. They are a dull white and a clutch usually consists of four to five. Normally two broods are reared in a season.

After nesting and prior to migration they collect in very large numbers, often with other martins and swallows, to roost communally in reed-beds. They are seldom seen to perch anywhere except on overhead wires, but infrequently they do land on the ground.

They feed on insects, mainly flies, which are caught in flight, usually over water. They are the smallest of the European swallows and are very gregarious at all times.

Easily distinguished by the earthy-brown upper parts, white underparts and brown breast band, in flight it does not show the white rump that the House Martin (*Delichon urbica*) does. It has a shallow forked tail and brown-black bill and legs.

Compared to the Swallow (*Hirundo rustica*) its flight is less graceful and much more flitting. Its weak twittering song is usually delivered whilst in flight, as are the calls. They are a brief 'tchirrip', and when alarmed a short 'pritt'.

Sand Martin in flight – note the band on the breast

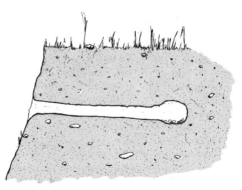

Section of a Sand Martin's nest tunnel

Swallow *Hirundo rustica*

Family: Hirundinidae

190 mm

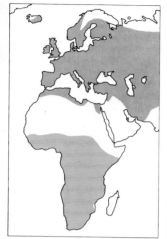

The Swallow is recognised as a typical migrant, spending the breeding season in Europe and travelling south in the autumn to winter in South Africa. Prior to the eighteenth century it was thought that Swallows overwintered in the bottom of muddy ponds, but this was disproved when a German ornithologist tied threads dyed with watercolours to some birds' legs. When they were examined the following year the colours were still visible, proving they had not been under water.

The Swallow is a bird of open cultivated country which performs aerial acrobatics to feed on flying insects, and hence they often congregate over open water, lakes and rivers. As they need to be constantly on the wing for feeding, they rarely perch except on wires and gutters near to the buildings in which they nest.

Its gregarious nature can be seen especially at times of migration, when large flocks gather prior to roosting communally in reed-beds. At other times they can be observed feeding in small flocks, especially over water.

It is distinguished by its long tail streamers, dark metallic-blue upper parts and neckband with chestnut-red throat and forehead. The underparts are variable from a rufous buff to creamy white. They have a thin black bill and legs. Juveniles appear in shape like the martins, lacking the long tail streamers of the adults. They, however, lack the brown colouring of the Sand Martin (*Riparia riparia*) and the white rump of the House Martin (*Delichon urbica*). The most common call is a high-pitched 'tswit, tswit, tswit' turning into an excited twittering. The song is a feeble twittering and warbling.

Even whilst nesting, Swallows tend to settle in groups, building their saucer-shaped nests on to a wall or on a beam in a farm or disused building. The nest is painstakingly constructed of mud bound together with a few pieces of grass. The lower picture shows a typical Swallow's nest. The saucer shape is open at the top unlike the House Martin's nest which is entered through a hole at the top. The nest is often used for as many as three broods in a season. The clutch of four or five eggs are white speckled with brown.

Swallow in flight – note the tail streamers

House Martin *Delichon urbica*
Family: Hirundinidae
130 mm

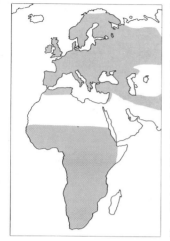

The House Martin is a fairly common summer visitor to the whole of Europe, arriving early in April to breed and returning to winter in southern Africa at the end of October.

It is normally found near human habitation or farm buildings but sometimes frequents rocky outcrops in more isolated places. As it is an aerial feeder flies, aphides and other small airborne insects are collected whilst on the wing, and hence a considerable time is spent in open country and over rivers and lakes.

It can easily be identified from other European Hirundines by its brilliant white rump and completely white underparts. Adults have blue-black upper parts, head, wings and tail. The short bill is black and the short legs and feet are covered in small white feathers. The short tail is forked. Both sexes are alike. Juveniles can be distinguished by their brownish-black upper parts.

The flight is similar to the Swallow's (*Hirundo rustica*) but is more fluttering. It is seldom seen perched on anything other than overhead wires and sometimes on rooftops. When nesting it alights near puddles to collect mud for building. Its usual flight call is a clear 'chirrip' or 'chichirrip', but when alarmed a shrill 'tseep'. The feeble but pleasant song is a twittering sound.

Nesting starts in early May when a mud nest is constructed under the eaves of a building or infrequently on a cliffside. Mud is collected in the bird's bill and mixed with saliva before being plastered in small globules to form the familiar cup-shaped nest. Unlike the Swallow's nest, the sides are continued right up to the eaves leaving an entrance hole in the wall at the top as shown in the lower right picture. Often old nests of previous years are patched up. Colonial nesting is very common and sometimes the colonies may be very large. Two broods are usually attempted each season, each clutch consisting of four or five glossy white eggs.

The House Martin's nest usually harbours large numbers of parasites, most abundant being the House Martin Flea (*Ceratophyllus hirundinis*). As many as 4,000 of these small fleas in larval and pupal form have been found in one nest. The fleas are, however, only found in small numbers on the adult birds and it is assumed that they are dependent on the young birds for their diet.

The small Moth (*Hofmannophila pseudospretella*) is found in larval form in many nests where it scavenges on faeces and nest rubbish.

The Common Louse-fly (*Ornithomya avicularia*) shown in the lower left picture is common on House Martins but is also found on many other bird species.

House Martin in flight – note the white rump and underparts

76

0 1 2 3 4 5 6 7 mm

Meadow Pipit *Anthus pratensis*
Family: Motacillidae
150 mm

A partial migrant, breeding in central and northern Europe and moving south-west for the winter. It breeds in open uncultivated country varying from the tops of mountains to rough pasture and even sand-dunes by the sea. In winter it prefers damp marshy areas, salt marshes and often cultivated land.

It is very similar to the Tree Pipit (*Anthus trivialis*) and can safely be distinguished in the field only by its call, a 'pheet-pheet-pheet'. The Tree Pipit's call is a loud harsh 'teeze'. Both have a song-flight with a 'parachute' descent but again there is quite a difference in sound. The Meadow Pipit's high-pitched notes increase in tempo until the call becomes a trill. Meadow Pipits' upper parts show great variability in colour from sandy buff through brown to olive-brown. Underparts are whitish flecked brown. Adults' legs are brownish flesh with a long hind claw. It is smaller and paler than the Rock Pipit (*Anthus spinoletta*).

Sexes are similar, but juveniles have pinker legs and more yellow plumage and can be confused with Tree Pipits.

The nest of fine grasses is usually well concealed in a tussock of grass. Four or five dirty white eggs with dense speckling of grey-brown are laid. It is normally double brooded.

Rock Pipit *Anthus spinoletta*
Family: Motacillidae   165 mm

Different subspecies of this bird occur throughout Europe, coastal races such as *A. s. petrosus* being called Rock Pipits and the mountain race *A. s. spinoletta* being Water Pipits.

Rock Pipits are birds of rocky coasts living on sandy and muddy shorelines in the winter. Water Pipits breed in barren rocky areas in mountainous districts and move south-west in the winter, visiting marshy areas in small groups. They are a little larger than Meadow Pipits (*Anthus pratensis*) and Tree Pipits (*Anthus trivialis*) and have a longer blackish-brown bill. The flesh-brown legs are darker in the Water Pipit. The Rock Pipit's upper parts are dark greyish olive-brown with darker streaks and the underparts are paler. It is the only Pipit with pale grey outer-tail feathers. The Water Pipit is similar, with a whitish eyestripe and white outer-tail feathers, but in summer it is quite different, the breast being a pinkish buff and almost clear of streaks. Usual calls are a thin 'tsip' or 'tseep'. The song is similar to the Meadow Pipit's and is usually part of a flight display. Four or five brownish speckled eggs are laid in a nest of grasses and moss lined with hair and finer grasses, situated in a grass tussock or rocky cavity.

Yellow Wagtail *Motacilla flava*
Family: Motacillidae   165 mm

The Yellow Wagtail is a summer visitor, well distributed throughout Europe apart from Scotland and Ireland. It occurs as several
different races, the Yellow (*M. f. flavissima*), as illustrated, breeds
in the British Isles and adjacent continental coastline. The
female duller than the male shown, being browner above and
paler below, although the males become dull in the winter.

The Blue-headed race (*M. f. flava*) is more prevalent in central
Europe. It has a blue-grey crown with darker ear coverts flecked
white, and white eyestripe and chin. The female is duller and
browner with a white chin. Other races are the Spanish Wagtail
(*M. f. iberiae*), from Iberia and southern France; the Ashy-
headed Wagtail (*M. f. cinereocapilla*), from Italy; the Grey-
headed Wagtail (*M. f. hunbergi*), from Scandinavia; and the
Black-headed Wagtail (*M.f. feldeggi*), from the Balkans. Many
variants occur, making subspecific identification very difficult.

They are usually found in damp situations, but also on dry
heath, moorland and agricultural land during migration. The
nest of grass and rootlets and lined with hair or feathers is
usually well hidden in a tussock near water. Four to six pale buff
spotted and blotched brown eggs are laid.

Pied Wagtail *Motacilla alba*

Family: Motacillidae   180 mm

Both European subspecies of this wagtail are partial migrants, with north-easterly birds wintering in southern Europe. The continental subspecies – the White Wagtail (*M. a. alba*) – however, migrates mainly to tropical Africa.

The picture shows a male of the British subspecies – the Pied Wagtail (*M. a. yarrellii*). It has a black back, breast, crown and throat and white forehead, cheeks and belly. The black tail has white outer feathers and the wings have two white bars. The female is greyer above and shows less black.

In winter both sexes can be confused with the White Wagtail when all have white throats and grey backs. In summer the male White Wagtail is distinguished by its pearl-grey back. All have black legs and a long tail which is continually 'wagged'. Juveniles have grey upper parts, whitish throat and breast with a small blackish bib.

The calls are a high-pitched 'tchizzik' and a sharp 'tchik'.

Their habitat is from open country to the centre of cities and often near water. The nest of twigs, grasses, roots and moss and lined with wool, hair and feathers is usually in a cavity. The three to seven eggs are whitish speckled or blotched grey.

81

Red-backed Shrike *Lanius collurio*
Family: Laniidae   170 mm

The Red-backed Shrike is a summer visitor to most of Europe apart from northern Scandinavia, northern British Isles, Iceland and southern Iberia. In autumn birds from western Europe take an unusual south-easterly route to their wintering grounds in South and East Africa. In recent years the Red-backed Shrike has been retracting its range and the number of birds breeding in western Europe is very much reduced.

The breeding habitat is either thorny scrub and hedgerows on sandy soils, or areas of light afforestation with widely scattered trees and thick undergrowth of thorn bushes, and sometimes sunny forest margins.

Like many of the shrikes, the Red-backed Shrike feeds on insects and small reptiles, mammals and birds. The prey is often impaled on its thorn-bush 'larder' until it is required, hence the popular name, 'butcher-bird'. The flight is direct but undulating, and when hunting it often hovers and glides. It is very fond of perching in prominent places awaiting its prey, and regularly wags its tail slowly from side to side. It is seldom seen on the ground, but when it is, it hops around.

The picture shows a pair displaying early in the breeding season. The male on the right is distinguished by its chestnut-brown back and blue-grey crown and rump. There is a broad black stripe through the eye to the rear of the ear coverts. The tail is black with white sides at the base. The underparts are pinkish buff. The female on the left has a duller chestnut-brown back and crown and the underparts are buffish with a mottling of crescent-shaped brown markings. Females usually lack the heavy black face markings. Juvenile plumage is similar to the female but has the crescent-shaped markings all over.

The hooked bill is black in the male and brownish in females and juveniles. The legs are greyish brown.

The harsh calls are a 'chack-chack' or 'chee-uk'. The song is a quiet warbling interspersed with various call notes.

The nest is almost always built in a prickly bush such as gorse, hawthorn, holly or brambles, but sometimes in young conifers. It is a cup-shaped construction of grasses, moss and plant stalks and lined with fine grasses, rootlets, hair and vegetable down.

The clutch size is usually from three to six and the colour is very variable. The eggs can be pale buff, pink, green or cream and have various marking from speckles, spots or blobs of red, brown, grey or olive. There is usually only one brood.

Waxwing *Bombycilla garrulus*
Family: Bombycillidae
175 mm

The Waxwing gets its name from the scarlet wax-like tips on its secondary wing feathers, although they are very much less evident on female and juvenile birds. Their plumage is mainly cinnamon-brown with distinct features of a pinkish-chestnut crest, black throat patch and eyestripe and bright yellow tip to the tail. The darker brown wings are heavily marked with white and yellow. Both the legs and bill are black. Juveniles have faint streaking on the underparts and lack the black throat patch.

They are stolid birds, with a strong but wavering flight. Their gregarious nature is seen as they move about in small parties and sometimes in large flocks during migration.

Breeding takes place in northern Scandinavia, with migration taking place into central and eastern Europe for the winter. In years when the availability of food at the breeding areas is good, the population is increased greatly and irruptions occur when substantial numbers arrive in western Europe as far south as Spain.

The breeding areas are in the vicinity of coniferous and birch woodland. Four or five eggs coloured pale blue with greyish and black spots are laid in a nest of twigs, mosses and lichen constructed in the branches of a tree.

Their diet consists mainly of berries and fruit. During the winter they roam the hedgerows and often move into parks and gardens performing acrobatic feats to get to their food. In open country they seem to prefer the fruits of hawthorn but in the garden cotoneaster and pyracantha are favourites. During the winter they become surprisingly tame, allowing one to approach within a short distance.

It is difficult to understand why the Waxwing was at one time called the Bohemian Chatterer, for it is fairly silent, with only a weak high-pitched 'sirrcee' as its call note.

Wren *Troglodytes troglodytes*

Family: Troglodytidae   95 mm

This tiny little bird is found throughout Europe except for northern Scandinavia. Over most of its range it is resident, but north-eastern populations move south and west to winter. It lives in all situations from remote rocky islands to suburban gardens, preferring the low cover of brambles in woods and thickets but making do with crevices in buildings, rocks and stone walls elsewhere.

It is easily identified in Europe as a very small bird with a short cocked-up tail. The upper parts, wings and tail are rufous brown with darker brown barring. The underparts are pale buffish to rufous with darker barring. In flight the wings appear very much darker brown than the rest of the plumage. The bill is brown and relatively long, slender and decurved, and the legs a lighter brown.

Wrens are extremely active, flitting amongst foliage or in old buildings to catch insects and spiders. Their flight is direct, and with fast wingbeats. On the ground they hop and creep about almost mouselike amongst the undergrowth in search of food.

The voice of the Wren is surprisingly strong for its size. Its song can be heard at almost any time during the year and is a passage of clear warbling intermixed with several more strident notes. When alarmed the usual call note 'tit-tit-tit' is prolonged into a harsh churring.

In the springtime the male constructs several nests about his well-defended territory. They are generally of globular shape and situated in crevices in trees, buildings or in hedges and haystacks. The materials used are small twigs, stalks, leaves and moss, but the final lining of hair and feathers is not added until a female has been accepted by the male in his territory and has chosen her preferred nest. The lower picture shows a typical nest built amongst roots in a bank. The unlined nests are used by the male for roosting.

During the winter it is not unusual for several wrens to use a nest as a communal roost, presumably to keep warm. Normally two broods of up to seven chicks are reared each season. The male cares for the first brood whilst the female incubates the second clutch of eggs. The minute eggs are white with tiny red-brown spots.

Dunnock *Prunella modularis*
Family: Prunellidae 150 mm

The Dunnock is often overlooked as just another sparrow, but it does not belong to the Sparrow family (Ploceidae) at all: it is a member of the Accentor family. At first sight it has a drab and somewhat featureless appearance, making it rather inconspicuous. It has rich brown upper parts streaked with darker brown, and dark grey underparts. The head and neck are grey with a dark brown crown and ear coverts. The legs are a flesh-brown and the thin bill is a blackish brown.

We usually see it on the ground searching for food, either hopping or shuffling along with jerky movements. Insects form the major part of its diet but in the winter it takes more seeds and sometimes berries. Although solitary, it is fairly abundant, frequenting almost any situation where there are bushes, hedges or scrubland with plenty of undergrowth. It is a common suburban bird and is even found in gardens well into large towns.

Its familiar call is a piping 'tseep' which often betrays its presence. It has a pretty little song very similar to the Wren (*Troglodytes troglodytes*) but shorter and less forceful. It sings throughout the year and sometimes during the night.

The nest is normally built at a height from ground level up to about four metres and is located in hedges, bushes and small trees; also occasionally in banks, haystacks and bundles of old garden rubbish. The neat little cup-shaped nest is constructed on a foundation of twigs with a mixture of grass, rootlets and moss. It is finished with a soft lining of hair, feathers, wool and moss. Two or even three clutches of four or five blue-green eggs are laid.

In Britain it is highly sedentary but birds from the north-eastern part of Europe do move south-west for the winter.

Whinchat *Saxicola rubetra*
Family: Turdidae
130 mm

The Whinchat winters in tropical Africa and is a summer visitor to most of Europe apart from northern Scandinavia, Iceland, southern Iberia and parts of Ireland and Italy.

It is similar to the Stonechat (*Saxicola torquata*) having a shortish tail but is not quite as plump and generally has a less upright stance. The upper parts, cheeks and crown are brown with dark streaks and the underparts are buff with a russet tinge on the breast and throat. The prominent eyestripe is white in the male and buff in the female and the tail feathers have conspicuous white patches at the base.

There is a white stripe from the chin down the sides of the throat and a small white wing patch. Females are generally paler and juveniles show no wing patches. The legs and bill are black.

Its breeding habitat varies somewhat but generally it prefers places where there are exposed perches and rough grassland. It is found in open country, common land, marshes, railway cuttings, and coastal warrens particularly where there are isolated bushes, gorse and bracken. On migration it is regularly seen in cultivated fields and coastal scrubland.

Like the Stonechat it likes to perch on the top of low bushes, posts and tall plants and similarly flicks its wings and tail.

The flight is flitting and it frequently indulges in flycatching. On the ground it hops.

The Whinchat's song is a short squeaky warble resembling that of the Redstart (*Phoenicurus phoenicurus*) or the Stonechat and is normally performed from a low perch.

Amongst the call notes are various clicking and churring noises but chiefly they are a 'tic-tic' or a 'u-tic-tic' usually accompanied by tail flicking.

The nest is usually very well hidden in a tussock of grass, sometimes under a bush and often amongst dead bracken. The main construction is of fine grasses on a base of rough grasses and moss. The lining is of fine roots and hair. Usually from four to six dark greenish-blue eggs are laid; occasionally they are finely speckled with brown at the fat end. Sometimes two broods are attempted.

Stonechat *Saxicola torquata*
Family: Turdidae

130 mm

The Stonechat is a partial migrant mainly confined to the British Isles and the southern and central parts of Europe. There is a general migration of birds from eastern and central Europe in southerly and westerly directions to wintering areas in Iberia and along Mediterranean coasts. It favours open coastal areas, common land, rough grassland, and marshland particularly where there are scattered low bushes and especially bracken and gorse.

The name Stonechat has been derived from its call, a harsh 'tsak-tsak' sounding like stones being hit together. Other calls are a 'weet, tsak-tsak' and 'tic-tic', similar to the Wheatear (*Oenanthe oenanthe*). The calls are usually accompanied by tail-flicking. The song, often resembling the Dunnock's (*Prunella modularis*), is an irregular series of squeaky notes delivered from a low but prominent perch or as part of its dancing song-flight.

The normal flight is low and flitting, with frequent attempts at flycatching. On the ground it hops and on perching it favours a prominent position on the top of a low shrub or on overhead wires. They sometimes move about in small family groups.

It has a more upright stance than the Whinchat (*Saxicola rubetra*). The male bird, as in the top picture, has a conspicuous black head and throat, white patches on its neck, rump and wings, brown upper parts and tail and a chestnut breast shading to a buff belly. After the autumn moult the male's plumage is much duller with the black parts showing brown. Females (as in the lower picture) and juveniles have very sombre plumage, being brown with darker streaks. They have a black bill and legs.

The breeding habitat is typically gorse, heather and bracken country and sometimes near young conifer plantations. The cup-shaped nest is mainly of grass with pieces of other nearby plants and bushes, and often odd materials like string, rags and paper are used. The preferred sites seem to be in gorse bushes or dead bracken but low bushes and brambles are used, and near the coast tussocks of grass or marram are used. When near the ground the nest is usually very well hidden.

Two broods per year are quite normal and often a third or even more is attempted.

A clutch usually comprises of from five to seven pale-blue eggs, speckled reddish brown at the fat end.

Wheatear *Oenanthe oenanthe*

Family: Turdidae

145 mm

The Wheatear is a summer visitor to Europe, occurring in most parts particularly during migration. Its breeding range is vast, covering most of Europe through Iceland and Greenland to Alaska. The Greenland race (*O. o. leucorrhoa*) breeds in Iceland, Greenland and the fringes of north-east Canada and passes through western Europe on migration. The wintering areas are in acacia steppe, savannas and on the bare ground throughout tropical Africa.

They are mainly birds of open country such as hill and moorland, preferring a breeding habitat where there are loose boulders, screes, stone walls and rabbit warrens. In many places they frequent disused quarries, sand-pits, sand-dunes and beaches.

They are habitually a ground bird, hopping about and frequently bowing and bobbing and waving their tails. In chasing around after flies they occasionally hover but generally the flight is flitting. Prominent rocks, walls, bushes and fences are regularly used as perches.

The rump and sides of the tail show as a brilliant white against the black tip and centre to the tail. The male in breeding plumage, as in the top picture, has a blue-grey crown and back, black ear coverts and broad white eyestripe. The underparts are shades of buff and the wings brownish black. In the autumn the males become more buffish with a browner back very much like the female in lower picture.

Juveniles are similar but have a more speckled plumage. The bill and legs are black.

The Greenland race has a slightly more upright posture and tends to be slightly larger with brighter underparts but it is generally quite difficult to distinguish the separate races out of the breeding season.

The calls are a rasping 'chack-chack' or 'weet-chack-chack'. The song, occasionally delivered in flight but generally from a prominent low perch, is a brief feeble warbling.

The nest is usually in a cavity under a boulder or in a rabbit's hole but often stone walls are used. Artificial nest sites made of bricks and tunnel-type nest-boxes sunk in shingle ridges as illustrated below have been very successful. The nest is of grass, roots and moss with a lining of hair, feathers, wool or rabbits' fur. Five or six pale-blue eggs occasionally speckled with brown spots are laid.

Tunnel-type nest-box used by Wheatears

Redstart *Phoenicurus phoenicurus*
Family: Turdidae

140 mm

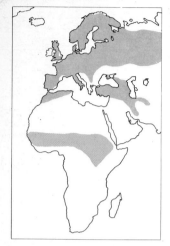

The Redstart is mainly a summer visitor to most of Europe apart from Ireland, Iceland and eastern Iberia. It returns to Europe towards the end of April after spending the winter in tropical Africa north of the Equator.

It frequents a habitat of wooded country heaths, parkland, orchards and large gardens and is regularly found around ruins and along slow-flowing rivers lined with pollard willows. In most places it seems to prefer a scattering of old trees.

Apart from the Black Redstart (*Phoenicurus ochruros*) it is the only small bird in Europe with a bright chestnut-red tail which is constantly flickered. The Nightingale (*Luscinia megarhynchos*) and Bluethroat (*Cyanosylvia svecica*) have chestnut-coloured tails but they are not nearly as bright.

The summer plumage of the male, seen in the picture, is outstanding with its slate-grey crown and upper parts, chestnut breast and flanks, black face and throat and white forehead. In autumn the black throat is flecked and fringed with white.

Females are less brightly coloured with grey-brown upper parts and buff underparts tinged pink on the breast. They lack the black and white markings of the males. Juveniles are paler still and are speckled like the juvenile Robin (*Erithacus rubecula*) but can be distinguished by the chestnut tail. Females and juvenile Redstarts are browner and paler than their Black Redstart counterparts. Male Black Redstarts are predominantly black or greyish black.

The bill and legs are black.

The flight is flitting and it frequently indulges in flycatching. On the ground it hops and behaves very much like the Robin.

Its song, usually performed from a perch high in a tree, is a hurried, squeaky little warble ending with a twittering sound.

Its calls include a warbler-like 'wheet', a 'whee-tuc-tuc' and a clear, sharp 'tooick'.

Nesting takes place in a hole or on a ledge in a tree or wall. Occasionally old Woodpeckers' holes are used and they readily accept nest-boxes in some areas. The nest consists of dry grasses, rootlets, moss and fibres of bark and is lined with feathers and hair. Five or six blue or greenish-blue eggs are laid; sometimes they are speckled with fine brown spots.

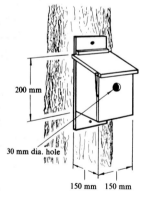

200 mm

30 mm dia. hole

150 mm   150 mm

Nest-box suitable for Redstarts

Robin *Erithacus rubecula*

Family: Turdidae

140 mm

Widespread throughout Europe except northern Scandinavia and Iceland. Birds from the northern and eastern parts of its range migrate to winter in southern and western Europe and North Africa. In Britain the Robin has become a symbol of Christmastime – the idea originating from Christmas notepaper on which a Robin was often depicted delivering the mail. It transpires that postmen at that time wore red uniforms and were nicknamed 'Robin'. In Britain during the winter the Robin often becomes very tame when in search for food – but elsewhere in Europe they are usually less confiding. The Robin is a bird from which many superstitions have arisen. Both sexes are very territorial; even the females hold territory in winter. Males become quite fierce in early springtime; however, the female is allowed to trespass to begin nesting as she takes the greater part in nest building whilst the male continues to defend his territory. They can be found in almost any place where there is suitable cover, such as woodland, hedgerows and shrubberies, and they have become common in the suburbs. Shelter is often sought inside buildings during hard weather.

The major part of their diet is taken up by grubs and small worms as can be witnessed when any soil is disturbed in the garden. They also take spiders and insects and in the wintertime are frequent visitors to bird-tables in search of kitchen scraps. They are very fond of suet and fanatical over mealworms. Mature birds have a rich orange-red breast and forehead and olive-brown upper parts. Both bill and legs are brown. The sexes are alike. Juveniles are quite different, lacking the orange altogether and being brown with pale buff mottling all over, as shown in the lower picture.

When moving on the ground the bird hops, often flicking its wings. Short wings contribute towards the 'flitting' type of flight. Robins sing throughout the year, often from a perch high in a bush. The song is defined as a series of short warbling phrases, bold in spring, but in winter, higher pitched and rather more fragile-sounding. Other calls are a 'tic, tic'; a high-pitched quiet 'tseee'; and a weak 'tsit'.

The Robin often nests in unusual places such as discarded pots and pans or inside old buildings. More generally it is in bushes or cavities in walls that the nest is built. It consists of grasses and moss with a feather lining and is often constructed on a base of dead leaves. The eggs, numbering from five to seven, are usually whitish, mottled with red-brown blotches and spots, but often the spots are so close that they give a reddish appearance.

An old watering-can makes an ideal nesting site

Nightingale *Luscinia megarhynchos*
Family: Turdidae   165 mm

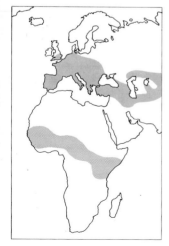

The Nightingale is a summer visitor preferring a habitat of deciduous woodland, or thicket with thick undergrowth.

The outstandingly rich song is perhaps the easiest way of recognising the species. It is melodious, loud and clear and usually performed from deep cover during day or night. The characteristic notes are repeated, such as 'chook-chook-chook' or 'pioo-pioo-pioo', the many phrases ending in a lovely crescendo. The main call notes are a whistling 'wheet', a 'tac-tac' and when alarmed a scolding 'kerr'.

Its movements are similar to the Robin (*Erithacus rubecula*), though being solitary and skulking it is seldom seen in the open, but when it is, it can be recognised by its chestnut-brown tail. The upper parts are rufous brown and underparts whitish brown. The bill is dark brown and legs are flesh to pale brown. Juveniles are distinguished by being paler and having mottled upper parts similar to juvenile Robins. Juvenile Redstarts (*Phoenicurus phoenicurus*) are smaller and have a brighter red tail.

Four or five olive-brown speckled eggs are laid in a nest of leaves and grass hidden on the ground in a hedge or under brambles.

Fieldfare *Turdus pilaris*

Family: Turdidae   250 mm

The most gregarious of the European thrushes, even nesting colonially. The Fieldfare breeds mainly in the north-east of Europe and migrates generally south-west for the winter. In winter it feeds in flocks mainly in open farmland, but as the weather turns harder it moves closer to human habitation, visiting orchards for fallen fruit, or hedgerows and large gardens where it feeds from berry-bearing shrubs. Fieldfares are then often seen in the company of Redwings (*Turdus iliacus*).

Seen at a distance it resembles the Mistle Thrush (*Turdus viscivorus*) but is slightly smaller. It can be distinguished by the blue-grey head and rump, rich chestnut-brown back and black tail. The underparts are buffish streaked and mottled with black. It has brown legs and a yellowish bill.

On the ground it has an alert upright posture and hops. The flight is in a straight line much the same as the Mistle Thrush. The wings are retracted every so often, missing a beat or so but without any undulation from the level path.

Its unmistakable call is a chuckling or laughing 'tchack-tchack' often uttered in flight. The song is a soft, very high-pitched, almost squeaking, warbling sound.

Blackbird *Turdus merula*

Family: Turdidae   250 mm

A very common bird, which has abandoned its once shy woodland habits to live closer to human habitation. The Blackbird prefers some cover such as small trees, bushes and shrubs but can also be found in wilder, uncultivated and open country. It is well distributed throughout Europe apart from northern Scandinavia. In autumn, considerable numbers of northern birds migrate southwards and westwards for the winter.

They feed on the ground, often running or hopping short distances and then stopping with head on one side listening for the movement of worms or insects. During autumn they supplement their diet with berries, and as winter approaches they can often be seen foraging in orchards for fallen fruit. They are regular winter visitors to gardens and bird-tables for the odd kitchen scraps they may pick up.

The Blackbird is a fine songster, its mellow fluting song, performed from a vantage point such as a tree or chimney, is varied and differs somewhat between individuals. The main call notes are the 'tchook, tchook, tchook' which turns into a chattering squeal when the bird is alarmed. When going to roost or whilst mocking or scolding some predator, a continuous 'pink-pink' call is uttered. When migrating, a high-pitched and vibrant note, very similar to that of the Redwing (*Turdus iliacus*), is often made.

Males, females and juveniles differ in plumage. Juveniles have a rufous mottled appearance as can be seen in the bottom left-hand picture. Immature males have a brownish-black plumage with blackish bills, whereas females, although similar, are more brown with brownish bill as can be seen by the bird feeding young in the bottom right-hand picture. The top picture shows an adult male Blackbird – they acquire the all-black plumage and bright orange-yellow bill when they are at least two years old.

It is not uncommon to see Blackbirds with partial or even all-white plumage. At all ages they have dark-brown legs. Flocking occurs on migration, but they also congregate together with other members of the thrush family whilst feeding during the winter.

Nesting occurs from early spring, some birds raising two or three broods and often using the same nest. The construction of the nest consists mainly of grasses and mud, often on a base of moss and lined with fine grasses. The sites are very varied, from trees and bushes to cavities or ledges in walls or banks. Very often unusual sites are chosen and unusual materials used. The nest in the picture was constructed of shredded paper in a printing factory. The usual clutch comprises from three to five blue-green mottled brown eggs.

Redwing *Turdus iliacus*

Family: Turdidae   210 mm

The Redwing is the smallest common thrush in northern Europe. It migrates to the south and west of Europe towards the end of October and early November, returning at the end of March. Its favourite wintering haunts are in open woodland, but as the weather becomes harder it moves closer to human habitation to feed on fallen fruit in orchards and berries from the hedgerows and shrubberies. At other times the diet consists mainly of worms, snails, insects and insect larvae.

It is very similar to the Song Thrush (*Turdus philomelos*), but is distinguished by the chestnut-red flanks and underwing and a prominent creamy-white eyestripe. The breast is buff streaked with brown and not spotted as in the Song Thrush. The upper parts are a uniform brown, the bill dark brown and legs a yellowish brown. Both sexes and juveniles have similar plumage. Redwings either hop or run and the flight is direct as in the Song Thrush.

Out of the breeding season the Redwing is highly gregarious, moving around in the company of Fieldfares (*Turdus pilaris*).

The song is not heard very often and tends to vary somewhat. Typically it consists of a phrase of four to six flute-like notes, 'trui-trui-trui-trui-trui-trui', interspersed and followed by a weak warbling subsong.

In flight, particularly during night migration, the distinctive but thin 'see-ip' call is given. Care must be taken in identifying night-migrating Redwings by this call as both Blackbird (*Turdus merula*) and Song Thrush have similar calls but they are less sibilant and higher pitched. Other calls are a soft 'chup', and when alarmed a harsh 'chittuck'.

The Redwing breeds in northern Europe but its range is expanding south and westwards. From early March nests are built, usually situated in trees and bushes but often old tree stumps and woodpiles are used. The nest habitat varies from open birch scrub to thick coniferous forest. In arctic tundra they are even found on the ground and often close to Fieldfare nesting colonies. The cup-shaped nest is constructed of twigs, roots and pieces of plant bonded together and lined with mud and fine grasses. From four to six eggs are laid. They are pale creamy green in colour with fine red-brown speckles becoming more dense at the larger end.

Redwings in flight

Song Thrush *Turdus philomelos*

Family: Turdidae

230 mm

The Song Thrush is a partial migrant found throughout Europe apart from southern Iberia and southern Italy. Northerly and easterly birds move south and west for the winter months. It is fairly abundant in mixed and deciduous woodland and is quite common around human habitation, favouring parks and gardens with hedges and bushes, and sometimes deserted outbuildings.

It can be distinguished from the Redwing (*Turdus iliacus*) by the lack of a prominent white eyestripe and by the fact that it has no chestnut colouring to the flanks or beneath the wings. Its size is much smaller than either the otherwise similar Mistle Thrush (*Turdus viscivorus*) or the Fieldfare (*Turdus pilaris*).

The upper parts are uniform olive-brown and the underparts a yellowish buff with small brown spots. Legs are flesh coloured and the bill brown. Juveniles have a yellow speckled mantle. The sexes are alike.

When on the ground it either runs or hops, often stopping with its head on one side listening for the movements of worms or insects. Small piles of broken snail shells can sometimes be seen around the countryside where the Song Thrush has brought snails to break them on a stone or rock – called its 'anvil' – to get at the juicy contents. Other food items include slugs and caterpillars, and in winter, berries and some fallen fruit.

The flight is fairly fast and direct. The flight call is a thin 'seep', similar but shorter than the Redwing's. A loud 'chook', similar to the Blackbird's (*Turdus merula*), is sometimes used and this is repeated rapidly when alarmed.

The song can be heard from late February and is usually performed from a high perch in a tree. The loud clear phrases, each repeated a few times, distinguish it from the other thrushes.

Song Thrushes are normally solitary but tend to flock on migration and associate with other thrushes when feeding during the winter. Nesting commences in early March, generally in hedges, bushes and small trees at a height between one and four metres. Occasionally ledges in buildings or on banks and cliffs are used.

The cup-shaped construction is of grasses and dry plant stems. British birds cement the inside with mud and saliva, the female moulding it to shape with her breast. Three to five blue-green eggs with fine black spots are laid.

106

Song Thrush's 'anvil'

Mistle Thrush *Turdus viscivorus*

Family: Turdidae   270 mm

The Mistle Thrush is distributed throughout the whole of Europe except northern Scandinavia. Many are residents but birds from north-eastern Europe tend to move south-west for the winter.

It can be found anywhere, from large gardens, orchards, woods and parkland to open country, but generally it prefers some scattered trees; it is normally quite shy. In winter it can often be seen on moorland and marshes.

Worms, insects and snails form the major part of the diet but during the autumn it turns to fruit and berries, particularly from rowan and yew trees and, of course, when they are available, the fruits of the mistletoe.

Male and female plumage are the same. Compared to other thrushes it has a more upright posture; it is much larger and paler than the Song Thrush (*Turdus philomelos*) and Redwing (*Turdus iliacus*), having greyish-brown upper parts, larger spots on the breast, and paler tail with whitish tips to the outer feathers. In flight it looks very much like the Fieldfare (*Turdus pilaris*), showing white under the wing and flying in a straight line, but the wing retractions are longer and more regular. The back is greyish brown and not like the Fieldfare, which has a chestnut back and a blue-grey rump.

The bill is brown and the legs yellowish brown. Juvenile birds have strongly spotted upper parts and have been confused with White's Thrush (*Zoothera dauma*). When on the ground it hops.

The Mistle Thrush sings in all weathers from tree tops, particularly conifers. The song is loud and very like the Blackbird (*Turdus merula*), but is more repetitive, lacking mellowness and variety and having pauses between phrases. In flight it has a harsh chattering call. It also has a call similar to the 'see-ip' of the Redwing and another hard 'tuc-tuc-tuc'.

Nesting usually takes place from early in March and often again in June. The nest is constructed of a mixture of grasses, twiglets and roots, and lined with mud and fine grasses. Generally four or five eggs are laid. They have a buff or bluish hue with brown spots and blotches.

Bearded Tit *Panurus biarmicus*
Family: Panuridae

170 mm

The Bearded Tit is distributed over central and southern Europe in many separate areas where suitable reed-beds occur. It is mainly resident but tends to wander during the winter. Seldom is it seen far from reed- and sedge-beds and seems to be dependent on extensive areas of reed and marsh, particularly in the winter. It is then highly gregarious, moving about in small parties feeding on insects and on the seeding heads of reeds (*Phragmites*). It is very 'tit-like' in its behaviour, particularly when swaying and climbing through the wind-blown reed-heads. It is the only small bird which has a long tail and confines itself to reed-beds.

Both sexes have light tawny-brown upper parts and tail and pale pinkish-grey underparts. The superb male is shown in the top picture, and is distinguished by his conspicuous black 'moustaches' and undertail coverts and a grey head. His wings are marked black and white. The lower picture of the female shows how she lacks all the distinctive markings of the male except on the wings. Juveniles are darker, particularly the underparts, wing-coverts and tail, but the throat is whitish. The bill is yellowish and the legs are black.

The flight is rather weak and undulating. It is very mouse-like when creeping around the base of the reeds in search of food but this it only does during the winter or when the wind is strong enough to prevent feeding in the reed-heads. Very often its presence is first given away by its piercing contact calls; a repeated 'cheeu, cheeu' or a metallic 'ching' and sometimes a soft 'pwut'.

Breeding usually starts around mid-April. The nest is constructed by both birds low down amongst dead reeds or thick sedge, generally in a swampy area adjacent a reed-bed, but sometimes amongst long dry grasses nearby. The materials used are dry reed leaves, grasses and sedge with a lining of fluff from the reed-heads. The eggs are white with spots and streaks of grey-brown. Two broods of from five to seven are usual but sometimes a third or even more are attempted.

Sedge Warbler *Acrocephalus schoenobaenus*
Family: Sylviidae   130 mm

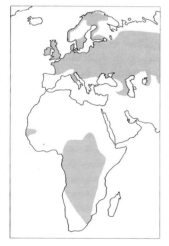

The Sedge Warbler is more often heard than seen as it performs its trilling and chattering song from amongst dense cover of a reed-bed or thicket, generally close to water. It also calls with a sharp 'tuc' and a harsh churring sound.

In early spring, before undergrowth becomes too thick it can often be seen early in the morning as it searches waterside trees and bushes for food. It is a small brown bird with bold darker-streaked upper parts and paler underparts. The rump is a plain rufous brown. It can be distinguished by the broad buff eyestripes from all other warblers except the Aquatic Warbler (*Acrocephalus paludicola*), which has an even more boldly striped head. Juveniles are more yellow with slight spotting on the upper parts of the breast. They have a buffish-striped head which could be confused with the Aquatic Warbler.

The nest is an untidy structure of moss and grasses in low dense vegetation and generally near fresh water. It is lined with feathers and other fluffy material. The clutch of five or six eggs are mottled yellow and brown with very fine black streaks.

It is well distributed over Europe apart from Iberia, southern France and central Scandinavia.

Reed Warbler *Acrocephalus scirpaceus*

Family: Sylviidae   130 mm

The Reed Warbler is a summer visitor to central and southern Europe arriving towards the end of April after spending the winter in Africa.

It is predominantly a bird of reed-beds and coarse vegetation near water. It is a social breeder often in the company of Sedge Warblers (*Acrocephalus schoenobaenus*). The superbly woven nest of grasses and reed tops is suspended amongst the stems of reed or other tall plants and varies from a simple cup to a deep conical shape. The lining is of fluffy reed-heads and sometimes hair, wool or feathers. Often two broods are attempted. The three to five eggs are a very pale green with varying amounts of dark grey, brown and olive blotches. The Reed Warbler's nest is often parasitised by the Cuckoo (*Cuculus canorus*).

The Reed Warbler's upper parts are brown with a rufous tinge. Underparts are whitish with buff tinges on breast and flanks. The thin bill is brown and the legs dark brown. Juveniles are more rufous with flesh-coloured legs.

The calls are mainly variations of 'churr'. The song is similar to that of the Sedge Warbler but is less varied and with phrases repeated. It sometimes mimics.

113

Garden Warbler *Sylvia borin*

Family: Sylviidae   140 mm

This bird is not especially found in gardens, particularly smaller gardens. It prefers a habitat of woodland, thicket, common or heathland where there is a substantial undergrowth of briars and brambles.

The Garden Warbler is a summer visitor to central and most of northern Europe, migrating in the autumn to winter in Africa south of the Sahara Desert.

It is fairly numerous, but its skulking habits and very(!) inconspicuous plumage account for it being relatively unnoticed. The plumage is rather sombre with no distinctive features. The upper parts are a uniform brown and underparts much paler. The head, however, has a characteristic shape, being rounder and having a stubbier bill than other similar warblers. The bill is brown and the legs are grey-brown, sometimes with a bluish tinge. In many ways it is like the female Blackcap (*Sylvia atricapilla*), but lacks the distinctive coloured crown. Its flight is also very similar, being erratic and flitting, and on the ground it hops.

The lovely, warbling song has similarities with the Blackcaps but is mellower, quieter and more sustained and usually performed from thick cover.

The calls consist of a harsh, low-pitched 'churr', a very soft 'whit' and a 'tac, tac' similar to the Blackcap but a little softer.

Its diet is mainly of insects but it does feed on some berries in the autumn.

Towards the end of April nesting starts, when a nest of grasses and moss is constructed low down amongst brambles and nettles. The lining is usually of finer grasses and rootlets, with a little hair. The four or five eggs are whitish buff with pale-brown blotches and some darker brown spots. Occasionally two broods are attempted.

Blackcap *Sylvia atricapilla*
Family: Sylviidae

140 mm

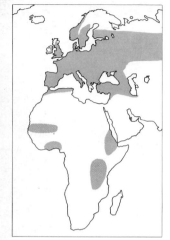

This species derives its name from the glossy black crown of the adult male bird as seen in the top picture. The female is shown below and is easily distinguished by its red-brown crown. The upper parts of both sexes are greyish brown but the female has browner underparts. Juveniles have browner upper parts and yellowish underparts as well as a red-brown crown. Juvenile males soon attain the black cap of the adults. The thin bill is blackish and the legs a dark grey.

The male bird can be mistaken for a Marsh Tit (*Parus palustris*) or Willow Tit (*Parus montanus*), especially when the latter is singing its warbler-like song, but both these birds are smaller and have black chins. The Sardinian Warbler (*Sylvia melanocephala*) and Orphean Warbler (*Sylvia hortensis*) also show a similarity but neither has the well-defined cap terminating at eye level, and each possesses white feathers in the tail.

The call notes are a 'churr' and a hard 'tac' similar to the Garden Warbler (*Sylvia borin*). The rich melodious and warbling song is also similar but is slightly higher pitched. It usually sings only when well hidden amongst undergrowth near its nest.

The preferred habitat is woodland and copses and tree-lined heathland with plenty of undergrowth and brambles. It seems to like evergreen shrubs, particularly rhododendrons.

The nest is built of dry plant stems mixed with wool and cobwebs, particularly on the rim. The lining is of very fine grasses and hair. It is sited amongst bushes and in hedges and often in brambles. The four or five eggs are a buffish colour blotched and speckled with various shades of brown and grey.

The young birds are fed on insects and smooth caterpillars but adults also consume insect larvae and spiders as well as soft berries. The Blackcap is numerous throughout Europe apart from northern Scandinavia and parts of Scotland and Ireland. It is a partial migrant with north-easterly populations moving south-west to winter, many going to West Africa.

Whitethroat *Sylvia communis*

Family: Sylviidae   140 mm

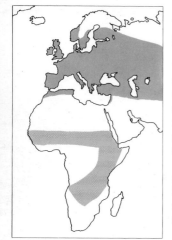

The Whitethroat, once abundant in Europe, has in recent years become affected by changes in climatic conditions in its wintering areas between the Sahara Desert and the Equator. The Sahel Zone has suffered a drought for several years, and birds which have depended on this area when they have migrated across the Sahara have arrived there only to find further desert conditions. The consequence is that many birds have perished and few have survived to return to Europe to breed. The wintering area of the Whitethroat extends down into eastern and southern Africa but here the birds are mainly races from east of the Mediterranean and eastern Russia.

It breeds over most of Europe apart from northern Scandinavia, Iceland and the northern isles of Britain. It prefers a breeding habitat of fairly open bushy country, commons, hedgerows and marginal land with plenty of low undergrowth such as nettles, brambles and gorse.

The nest is generally very well hidden, low down in thick undergrowth where there is dead vegetation for support. The cup is built from fine dry grass stems with odd leaves and pieces of moss and adorned with pieces of fluffy material. The lining is of fine rootlets and hair.

Normally four or five eggs are laid. They are buffish with yellow-grey and brown spots.

After breeding it sometimes joins up in small parties with other warblers foraging in the trees.

The pictures show the male above and female below. Both are showing typical display postures early in the breeding season. The male has a pure white throat and grey cap which becomes brownish in the autumn. The wings are rufous brown, the underparts buff, and the brown tail has white outer feathers. The female is not so bright and has a brownish head. Juveniles are similar to the female but have only a dirty white throat. The thin bill is a greyish brown and the legs pale brown. It has a skulking behaviour but can often be seen flitting in and out of the undergrowth. Its flight is the flitting typical of warblers.

Amongst its calls it has a harsh scolding 'tcharr', a quiet repeated 'whit-whit-whit' and a repeated 'tac, tac'. The jangling song is often uttered as the bird 'parachutes' down from a display flight over its territory.

Willow Warbler *Phylloscopus trochilis*

Family: Sylviidae   110 mm

This common summer visitor is most abundant in northern Europe when it returns in April from wintering in tropical and southern Africa.

It can normally be found hopping and flitting around in the higher branches of trees and bushes searching for small insects and spiders. It seems to prefer thick and mixed deciduous woodland but is also found in coniferous forest and heathland. It has no special preference for willows.

The plumage of male and female is alike and is pale greenish olive-brown with pale buffish-yellow underparts. The legs are usually light brown, but this is unreliable for identification as some birds have flesh-coloured legs whereas others have dark brown. (However, we can say that a bird with flesh-coloured legs is a Willow Warbler.) The thin bill is brown. The Willow Warbler is very similar to the Chiffchaff (*Phylloscopus collybita*) and can only safely be distinguished from it by its song. The underparts have a yellower tinge (particularly obvious in juveniles in autumn) when compared to the whitish underparts of the Chiffchaff. Even so the situation is complicated by two colour forms of the northern race of Willow Warbler. One is identical to the southern breeding birds and the other is browner above and whiter below.

Birds trapped for ringing and study are distinguished by their wing formulae. The Willow Warbler has a longer second primary equal in length to the fifth, and has no emargination on the sixth. This can be seen in the sketch on page 122.

The call note is a quiet 'hooeet', not unlike the call of the Chiffchaff or Redstart (*Phoenicurus phoenicurus*). The song is quite unlike the Chiffchaff's. The series of descending notes starts off very quietly increasing in volume and finishing on a rippling flourish – 'sooeet-sooeetoo'.

The Willow Warbler's song is undoubtedly the commonest bird song in woodlands from the time when it arrives in April to late May. At this time a neat dome-shaped nest is constructed on or close to the ground in a clump of grass or heather. It consists of grasses and leaves and is interwoven with mosses. Usually six or seven pinkish-white eggs speckled pink and brown are laid.

In the autumn Willow Warblers and Chiffchaffs can often be seen amongst small parties of tits.

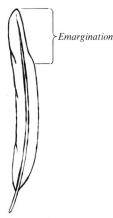

Emargination

Emarginated feather

120

Chiffchaff *Phylloscopus collybita*

Family: Sylviidae

110 mm

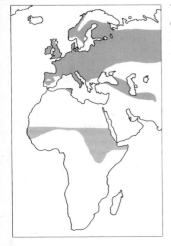

The Chiffchaff is one of our earliest summer visitors, arriving early in March from its winter quarters in Africa and along the Mediterranean coast. Its breeding distribution covers most of Europe apart from areas of northern and southern Scandinavia, Scotland and Iberia.

It is very similar to the Willow Warbler (*Phylloscopus trochilis*) and they can only safely be identified in the field by their quite different songs. The Chiffchaff, however, has a more rounded shape and its plumage appears less green above and paler below. The legs are usually a dark brown, whereas most Willow Warblers have light-brown legs; however, this cannot be used as a positive distinction between the two species. The thin bill is blackish.

The sketch shows a comparison of Chiffchaff and Willow Warbler wing formulae. Birds trapped for ringing can be identified in this way – the Chiffchaff having its second primary shorter than the sixth and the sixth primary emarginated.

Its movements are very restless as it hops from branch to branch flicking its wings and tail. It has a flitting flight.

One of its calls is also similar to the Willow Warbler. It is a soft 'hooeet'. Others are a sharp 'twit' and a quiet 'chiff, chiff, chiff'.

The song is very distinctive consisting of two notes repeated several times in irregular order, 'chiff, chaff, chiff, chiff, chaff . . .'. It is usually performed from tree tops around five metres from the ground.

The preferred habitat is thin woodland and small copses with thick undergrowth.

The nest is usually constructed in low undergrowth where the bushy growth adjoins herbal vegetation, but often in isolated bushes. It is a rather untidy collection of dead leaves and grasses intermixed with moss and fibrous materials. The lining is of feathers and a little hair.

From four to seven, but generally six eggs are laid. They are white with purple-brown spots. Often two broods are attempted.

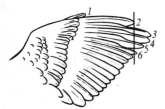

Chiffchaff

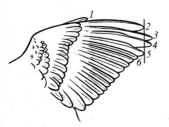

Willow Warbler

Note that the Chiffchaff's sixth primary is emarginated and the second primary is shorter than the Willow Warbler's.

Goldcrest *Regulus regulus*

Family: Regulidae

90 mm

This pretty little bird is distinguished from the warblers and tits by its small size (it is even smaller than the Wren (*Troglodytes troglodytes*) and weighs only five grammes) and by its bright yellow crest bordered with black. Adult males show a bright orange centre to the raised crest. Apart from this, both sexes appear the same, having olive-green upper parts and pale whitish-buff underparts. The wings show two white bars separated by a dark greenish-black band. The thin bill is black and the legs brown.

It can easily be distinguished from the Firecrest (*Regulus ignicapillus*) by the lack of black and white eyestripes.

It is well distributed over most of Europe and can be found particularly in coniferous and mixed woodland. It also inhabits large gardens, parks, common and heathland, particularly where there are scattered trees and shrubbery.

The song is a thin high-pitched 'ceda-ceda-ceda-ceda-cissa-pee'. The call most frequently heard is a thin 'zee-zee-zee', which could easily be confused with either Tree Creeper (*Certhia familiaris*) or Coal Tit (*Parus ater*).

Its behaviour is very warbler-like. Outside the breeding season it can be seen in small flocks often accompanied by tits. The flight is undulating, resembling that of the tits. It is very seldom seen on the ground.

The Goldcrest is generally a resident bird but many northern birds move to southern or western Europe for the winter. Nesting takes place from early April, when a suspended nest of woven grasses, mosses, lichen, hair and spiders' webs is constructed, usually under the tip of a conifer branch. The round basket-shaped nest has a very narrow entrance hole at the top and is normally well concealed. The clutch of eggs varies from seven to eleven in number; they are a buff-white colour mottled with small brown spots, especially round the large end. The Goldcrest's diet consists entirely of spiders, small caterpillars and insects, particularly flies, but during the winter they depend a lot on insect eggs and pupae.

Firecrest *Regulus ignicapillus*

Family: Regulidae
90 mm

The Firecrest is a partial migrant breeding mainly in south-western Europe, but has in recent years extended its range northwards into southern England. Many birds in the north-eastern part of the range move southwards and westwards for the winter.

It is found in coniferous and mixed woodland, particularly where there is low undergrowth, and sometimes in thickets, overgrown brambles or bracken.

In many ways it is similar to the Goldcrest (*Regulus regulus*) but can be distinguished by the white stripe above the eye and the black stripe through it. The upper parts are a slightly darker olive-green and the whitish buff underparts are whiter than the Goldcrest's. The sides of the neck are tinged bronze. The sexes are alike, having an orange crest similar to the male Goldcrest. Juveniles lack the crest but show signs of the black and white stripe on the head.

It is rarely seen on the ground and has a weak undulating flight similar to the tits. Out of the breeding season it is often in the company of tits and Goldcrests.

The calls – a low 'zit' or a 'zit, zit' – are similar but less penetrating than the Goldcrest's.

Dependent on the preferred habitat of birds in different areas, the nest site varies somewhat. Nesting in some places is high in the branches of conifers but deciduous trees are also used. Nests have been located in creepers and bushes, particularly in Iberia.

The nest itself is a tiny basket of moss bound together with spiders' webs and often interwoven with small twigs and conifer needles. The lining is of feathers. From seven to twelve pale pinkish-buff eggs with pale-brown speckles are laid. Two broods are often attempted.

Spotted Flycatcher *Muscicapa striata*
Family: Muscicapidae   140 mm

This summer visitor is well distributed throughout all of Europe apart from the northernmost part of Scandinavia and Iceland. It migrates from its wintering quarters in southern Africa to arrive in Europe in late April or early May. Its breeding habitat is very varied, from sub-arctic birch woods and tall forests to mixed woodland, orchards, parks and gardens.

Spotted Flycatchers choose varied sites for their nests, including the upper side of a branch next to a tree trunk, the space behind creepers on a wall, rafters in old buildings and ledges over doorways or on the sides of buildings in towns. Sometimes they use an old nest left by other birds. The nest construction is a fairly flimsy affair of moss, grasses, leaves and fibrous materials formed into a flat cup shape. The outside often has odd bits of paper, cloth and cobweb hanging from it, while the lining is of fine rootlets or hair with some feathers. Usually four or five eggs are laid. They are from pale blue to greyish blue with varying amounts of reddish-brown spots and streaks. Sometimes two broods are attempted.

They are aerial feeders, depending on flying insects for their diet. Only very occasionally do they fly to the ground to pick up insects. It is more usual to see them waiting on a low perch for some insect to fly past; then they dart out to catch it and return to the same place. They regularly flick their tail and wings when perched.

When in sustained flight they have a fairly fast and slightly undulating movement. The characteristic upright posture is typical of flycatchers.

The plumage is mainly greyish brown on the upper parts and the underparts are much paler with darker fine streaking on the crown and breast. Juveniles have a more mottled appearance. Both sexes have similar plumage. The very short legs and the bill are blackish.

When alarmed it calls a rapid 'twee-tuc-tuc'. Its main call is a thin, shrill 'tzee'.

The song is a rapid series of shrill, squeaky and often feeble notes which are somewhat unrecognisable as a song.

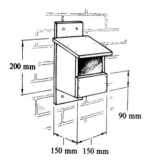

200 mm

90 mm

150 mm   150 mm

Open-fronted nest-box suitable for Spotted Flycatchers

Long-tailed Tit *Aegithalos caudatus*
Family: Paridae
140 mm

The tail of the Long-tailed Tit is over half its overall length. This feature and the black, white and pinkish plumage and distinctive calls make it easy to identify. The British race (*A. c. rosaceus*) as illustrated is similar to the western and southern European races, but having a whitish head with a prominent black stripe over the eye. The underparts are white tinged pink on the belly and undertail coverts and the upper parts are black and pink. The orbital ring and eyelids are pink and the bill is black. Adults have dark-brown legs whereas juveniles have pale brown. Juveniles' plumage lacks the pink colouring. The northern European race (*A. c. caudatus*) lacks the black stripe over the eye and has an all-white head, throat and underparts.

Although very acrobatic, its flight is weak. Out of the breeding season it usually moves about in small family parties.

The calls are a 'tupp', a repeated 'tsirrup' and 'si-si-si'.

It is found mainly in woodland, hedgerows and bushy commons.

The beautiful nest is an oval shell of moss, cobwebs and hair lined with large numbers of feathers and covered outside with pieces of grey lichen. The entrance is usually at the top. From seven to twelve white eggs with a few red speckles are laid.

130

Marsh Tit *Parus palustris*

Family: Paridae   110 mm

The Marsh Tit, contrary to what its name implies, has no special preference for marshland and is found not only in damp woodland but also in woodland, thickets and hedgerows well away from water. It is a shy, rather solitary little bird which is easily confused with the Willow Tit (*Parus montanus*) but can be distinguished by its call – a loud 'pitchue' or 'pitchuee' and sometimes a scolding 'chicka-pee-pee-pee'. It does, however, have one call – a harsh 'tchair' – not unlike the Willow Tit. Its build is also slightly different, its neck being slimmer and it shows no signs of a pale wing panel or patch.

The plumage is brown with a black cap and chin. Underparts and cheeks are paler. The legs are blue-grey and the bill black. Juveniles appear to have greyer upper parts with a sooty crown and are virtually indistinguishable from juvenile Willow Tits. It hops along the ground and the weak flight is undulating. In winter odd birds often accompany small tit flocks.

Nesting occurs from early April to mid June. The usual site is a hole or crevice in a tree or post but occasionally in a wall. Very rarely do they excavate their own hole. Six to eight white eggs with fine red-brown spots are laid.

131

Willow Tit *Parus montanus*
Family: Paridae   115 mm

Willow Tits are distributed over most of Europe except for Italy, Iberia, Ireland and parts of Scotland. Sporadic movements occur when northern birds arrive in central Europe to winter.

They favour damp deciduous woodland and thicket, particularly where the land is marshy, with no special preference for willows. The Willow Tit is almost identical to the Marsh Tit (*Parus palustris*), but is distinguished by its individual call and the pale edges to the secondaries appearing as a light patch. The black bib usually appears larger and the neck thicker. It has a black cap and brown upper parts. The underparts and cheek patches are greyish white to buff. The northern race (*Parus m. borealis*) is generally paler and whiter.

The characteristic calls are a harsh loud 'chay-chay-chay', a thin 'eezeez-eez' and 'si-si-si'. The warbling song is seldom heard and consists of a mixture of high-pitched squeaky notes amongst a more liquid song similar to the Wood Warbler's (*Phylloscopus sibilatrix*) 'piu-piu-piu'.

Breeding occurs in marshy areas where the birds excavate their own nest holes in rotten trees. Six to nine white eggs speckled pink are laid.

Crested Tit *Parus cristatus*

Family: Paridae   110 mm

Common throughout Europe apart from England, Ireland, Italy and northern Scandinavia. It is found more frequently in pine-woods but also occurs in mixed woodland.

It is easily identified by its obvious black and buff speckled crest. The upper parts are a warm brown and the underparts pale buff to white. The brown wing has no wing bars. The cheeks are white with a black stripe from behind the eye and curving round to border the ear covert. A narrow black collar curves round to join up with the black bib. The bill is black and the legs grey. The sexes are alike.

It feeds mainly on small insects, spiders and beetles which it searches out from the tree foliage. It also feeds on small seeds. The distinctive call is a short trilling 'choo-r-r', also a repeated 'tsee-tsee-tsee'.

The nest is usually situated in a hole in a rotten tree, but it will use nest-boxes. Up to ten pinky-white eggs speckled with red-brown spots are laid. Occasionally a second brood is attempted.

After nesting Crested Tits roam the woodland in small groups, often in the company of other tits.

133

Coal Tit *Parus ater*

Family: Paridae   110 mm

Spread throughout Europe apart from northern Scandinavia and Iceland. It is resident in the south-west but sporadic migrations of north-eastern birds to central Europe do occur.

It can easily be distinguished from the other black-capped tits by the conspicuous white patch on the nape and the unmarked whitish-buff breast. The upper parts are olive-grey and the black bib stretches from the chin to the upper parts of the breast. It has dirty white cheek patches, thin double white wing bar, pale slate legs and black bill. Continental birds usually appear brighter coloured. Juveniles have a yellowish tinge to the white markings of adults and could be confused with juvenile Great Tits (*Parus major*), which are bulkier and have yellowish breasts.

The Coal Tit can be found mainly in woodland and farmland with scattered trees, particularly where conifers are present. The song is a clear repetitive 'seetoo-seetoo'. When alarmed it scolds 'chi-chi-chick'. Other calls such as the thin 'tsee' or 'sissi-sissi-sissi' resemble the other tits and Goldcrest (*Regulus regulus*).

The nest in a tree cavity or hollow stump is lined with moss and hair. Sometimes rock crevices are used and they also use nest-boxes. A clutch of about ten white eggs speckled brown are laid.

Blue Tit *Parus caeruleus*

Family: Paridae   115 mm

Blue Tits are found in woods, copses and gardens and are often common in city parks. In winter some become quite tame, coming into gardens for food, whilst others form small flocks feeding on insects in reed-beds. In the autumn it forms up in parties with other tits, Goldcrests (*Regulus regulus*) and warblers feeding in the tree canopy.

Being very acrobatic, it is able to feed in almost any position, thriving on nut feeders and at bird-tables. When on the ground it hops. The weak flight tends to be undulating.

Adults have bright cobalt-blue on the head, wings and tail; a pale yellow-green mantle and yellow underparts and white patches on the cheeks and nape. The legs are dark blue-grey and the bill black. Juveniles are much duller, being more yellowish generally with greenish-brown upper parts (see left-hand picture).

The variety of calls is characteristic of the tit family, but most typical is a scolding 'tsee-tsee-tsee-tsit'.

Nesting in holes in trees, wall cavities and nest-boxes, it lays up to fifteen or more small white eggs with pink speckles in a nest of moss, wool and feathers.

135

Great Tit *Parus major*

Family: Paridae   140 mm

The largest of the tit family, the Great Tit is found mainly in deciduous woodland and often in rural gardens and parks. After breeding it becomes very sociable, mixing with small flocks of other tits and warblers feeding on insects in trees and hedgerows. In winter it often visits bird-tables and tends to dominate nut feeders.

It can be recognised by its black head with white cheek patches and the black bib down the centre of its yellow underparts. Juvenile birds are more yellow all over, the black parts being brownish until the first moult.

Like most of the tit family it has a weak undulating flight. When on the ground it hops.

The main call is a high-pitched metallic sound similar to the 'pink' of the Chaffinch (*Fringilla coelebs*). The short, high-pitched two-or-three-syllable song 'teachew-teachew' is more often uttered during springtime from a tree-top song post.

The nest is built of moss and hair in holes in trees, wall cavities or nest-boxes. From five to twelve or more eggs are laid. They are white speckled with small pinkish-grey spots.

Nuthatch *Sitta europaea*

Family: Sittidae   140 mm

Normally a resident, distributed throughout Europe except northern Scandinavia, Ireland and Scotland, the Nuthatch is common in woodland where old deciduous trees are present. It is a thick-set little bird with a strong pointed bill and short stubby tail, most often seen climbing up or down trees in short jerky movements, searching for insects. It is very partial to small nuts which it breaks open after wedging them in bark crevices.

Nuthatches are the only small tree-climbing birds with blue-grey upper parts and pale-buff to chestnut underparts (the British race has more chestnut underparts). They have a black stripe through the eye and white cheeks and throat. Sexes are similar but males show more chestnut on the flanks. Juveniles lack all chestnut colouring.

The loud calls range from a ringing 'chwt-chwit-it' or a sibilant 'tsirr' to a tit-like repetitive 'tsit'. The song is a repeated 'tui' or a two-syllable piping 'quee-quee, quee-quee'.

The nest is usually in a tree cavity or wall crevice or sometimes in a nest-box. The entrance and any cracks are plastered with mud. The six to ten eggs are creamy white spotted with red, brown and grey.

Tree Creeper

Short-Toed Tree Creeper

Entrance hole each side 20 mm wide by about 50 mm long

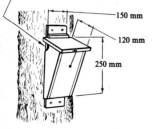

150 mm

120 mm

250 mm

Wedge-shaped nest-box suitable for Tree Creepers

Tree Creeper *Certhia familiaris*
Family: Certhiidae   130 mm

The Tree Creeper is mainly resident in the British Isles, much of Scandinavia and eastern Europe but is absent from most of Iberia, France, Belgium and Holland and the Mediterranean coast. In southern Europe, however, the Short-Toed Tree Creeper (*Certhia brachydactyla*) is resident and their ranges overlap somewhat.

Being very similar in appearance and behaviour they are most difficult to distinguish in the field apart from obvious differences in voice. They are small birds with thin curved bills and climb spirally up trees with their stiff tail supporting them. The creeping movement is very mouse-like and intermittent with pauses to search in bark crevices for insects. They have a weak undulating flight and rarely fly any appreciable distance.

The upper parts are brown with buff streaks but when compared the Short-Toed Tree Creeper has a greyer appearance as can be seen in the right-hand picture. The underparts are a silvery white and the legs and bill are brown.

The lengths of bill and claws are unreliable factors in distinguishing the two species, even when in the hand, as there is a considerable overlap in dimensions owing to variations within each of the species.

Their habitat is woodland, parks and gardens where there are large trees, although the Short-Toed Tree Creeper seldom occurs in thick woodland.

Occasionally family parties move about together, particularly in the autumn. In the winter the odd bird often accompanies parties of tits and Goldcrests.

The most reliable factor in distinguishing between the two species is their voice. The Tree Creeper's calls are a thin, high-pitched and drawn-out 'tsee' and a 'tsit' very much like the calls of tits. The song, also weak and high pitched, resembles 'tee-tee-tee-tsissiooee'.

The Short-Toed Tree Creeper has a loud piping 'srrieh' call. The song resembling 'teet, teet, teeteroitit' is lower pitched and sounds richer than the Tree Creeper's song.

Typical nest sites are behind loose bark on trees but cavities in building and special nest-boxes are often used. The nest, on a foundation of twigs, is made of moss, roots and grass with pieces of fibrous bark and a lining of feathers, hair or wool.

Both species lay five to six eggs of similar coloration. They are white with a zone of red-brown spots at the fat end and Short-Toed Tree Creepers' eggs often have additional fine red-violet speckles in the same zone. Two broods are often attempted.

138

Corn Bunting *Emberiza calandra*

Family: Emberizidae   180 mm

The Corn Bunting is the largest of the Buntings in Europe. Its range covers most of central and southern Europe but it is absent from Iceland, Ireland and some isolated areas in the south of the range. It is seldom seen in Sweden and Norway and many birds from the northern part of the range migrate south for the winter.

Its size, plump appearance and its habit of flying with its legs dangling distinguish it from all other small birds with non-descript plumage. It is golden brown with darker streaks above and below, yellow legs and a yellow-horn bill and a brownish cleft tail. Both sexes have similar plumage. The flight seems laboured and is usually direct but often undulating. When on the ground it normally hops but occasionally it runs. It is fond of perching on posts and overhead wires and during the breeding season several favourite song perches may be used. These are usually prominent stems on bushes or tall plants near to the nest.

Often males are polygamous, taking on two or more females with nests only a short distance apart. Nesting starts in mid May in fairly open country or farmland with a few scattered trees. Usually the breeding habitat is an open area such as rough farmland or an old airfield with low bushes or gorse and brambles.

The nest site is normally adjacent to some prominent plant such as a thistle or a large tussock of grass which can be used as a song perch. The nest, a loose construction of grass lined with fine rootlets and hair, is usually positioned in a scrape on the ground or occasionally low in a bush.

From three to five eggs are laid. The colours are very variable. Normally they are a very pale lilac streaked and blotched heavily with dark-brown markings, but sometimes the basic colour is anything from white to pale red-brown. Two broods, and some-times three, are often attempted.

The Corn Bunting's song is short and high pitched, sounding like the jingle of a bunch of keys. Its calls which are often uttered in flight are a short 'chip' or 'chip-a-chip' and a harsh drawn-out 'zeep'.

Yellowhammer *Emberiza citrinella*

Family: Emberizidae

165 mm

Throughout the greater part of Europe apart from the Mediterranean coast, northern Scandinavia and Iceland, the Yellowhammer is fairly common. It is a partial migrant with northern populations moving south for the winter.

Its habitat is typically open country with hedgerows and bushes. It tends to avoid human habitation except when it visits farmyards and stubble fields in the winter in search of fallen seed. It is more often found along roadside hedgerows, on bushy commons and heathland, in young conifer plantations and on bracken-covered hillsides. The male as seen in the top picture is distinguished by being the only finch-like bird in Europe with a yellow head and underparts and a chestnut rump. The upper parts are chestnut with darker streaks.

Females as shown in the lower picture and juveniles are not so bright yellow and are browner with darker streaks on the head. The chestnut rump distinguishes them from the Cirl Bunting (*Emberiza cirlus*) which has an olive-brown rump.

The white outer feathers of the brown cleft tail are very obvious at all ages, especially in flight. The legs are a pale brown and the bill a pale grey-brown.

The main diet is seeds but they also eat insects, worms and spiders particularly during the breeding season when they are feeding young.

It hops or occasionally runs when on the ground. The flight is direct and sometimes undulating.

After breeding it becomes highly gregarious, forming up in flocks with other seed-eating birds, especially the House Sparrow (*Passer domesticus*), Chaffinch (*Fringilla coelebs*) and Greenfinch (*Carduelis chloris*), to feed on stubble fields.

The song, often expressed as 'little-bit-of-bread-and-no-cheese' is a rapid high-pitched 'ch-chi-chi-chi-chi-chweee' and is regularly performed in springtime from high in a hedgerow or bush.

The flight call is a metallic 'twitup'. Others are a 'chip' or a 'twink'.

A substantial nest of straw and grass often with a little moss is built low in a hedge, tree or bank particularly where there is a good undergrowth of grass. Often sites in brambles or bracken or even haystacks are used.

From three to five eggs are laid. They are whitish toned with pale purple or red-brown and have varying amounts of dark spots or streaks. Two broods, and often three, are attempted each year.

Reed Bunting *Emberiza schoeniclus*

Family: Emberizidae

150 mm

Widely distributed throughout Europe apart from Iceland, the Reed Bunting is a partial migrant with north-easterly populations moving into south and western Europe for the winter.

At one time this was a bird of reed-bed, marsh and fenland but it is increasingly resorting to rough grassland, heaths, hedgerows and young conifer plantations particularly in Britain. During the winter it regularly takes to farmland, especially stubble fields, in search of fallen seeds. It is also found amongst coastal marram grass and at flooded gravel-pits.

The plumage is mainly brown with darker streaks, the rump is greyish brown and the cleft tail has conspicuous white outer feathers. The underparts are greyish white with black streaks on the flanks.

The male in breeding plumage, as in the top picture, is distinguished by his black head and throat and a white collar, but in the winter these distinct markings are obscured by brown mottling. He can be confused with the male Stonechat (*Saxicola torquata*) but that is smaller and lacks the white in the tail.

Females, as in the lower picture, and juveniles have an all-brown head with a buff eyestripe and throat. They have a pale buff moustachial stripe contrasting with the darker ear coverts above and a black flecking below. The rump is browner than the adult male's. Legs and bill are dark brown.

It is a lively bird, hopping, walking or running when on the ground. It is very agile when flitting through reed-beds and hanging on to reed stems. The flight is undulating and twisting.

The song is usually performed from a high reed stem or bush and is a repeated squeaky 'tweek, tweek, tweek, tississick'.

The calls are a loud 'tseep' or 'tsink' and when alarmed a spitting 'chit'.

After breeding it becomes gregarious, often accompanying other buntings and finches. In spring it is often seen with Meadow Pipits (*Anthus pratensis*) on migration.

Nesting usually takes place in damp situations near water, but occasionally in quite dry places. The site is normally near the ground amongst tussocks of sedge or rushes but also in briars, osier beds, hedgerows and gorse. A bulky nest of sedge or dry grass is lined with hair or fine grass and sometimes with down from reed-heads.

Four or five eggs are laid. They are usually buff or to a pale greeny brown with brown streaks, spots and blotches. Two broods are normal and sometimes a third is attempted.

Chaffinch *Fringilla coelebs*
Family: Fringillidae

150 mm

Possibly the commonest finch in Europe, it is found almost everywhere except the most northern part of Scandinavia. Birds from the far north migrate south towards the Mediterranean for the winter, returning in early March.

A typical adult male is shown in the top picture and the female below. Comparing the Chaffinch with other birds of similar size, it is easily distinguished by the white patch on the shoulder and the white wing bar just below it. The Hawfinch (*Coccothraustes coccothraustes*) is twice the size and has a much larger bill. The outer-tail feathers are also white. Males have the crown and nape a slate-blue colour, a chestnut-coloured mantle with greenish rump and pinkish-brown underparts. The bill is blue-grey in summer but turns pale brown in the winter. Females and juveniles are more soberly coloured, being pale olive-brown above with paler underparts and having a brown bill. The legs are a pale brown.

On the ground it either hops or walks. The flight is bounding, with the white shoulder patches showing very clearly.

It can be found in almost any situation where there are trees and bushes from mature woodland, copses and hedgerows to commons, parks and gardens. It is fairly common in suburban gardens. Except when breeding it is very gregarious and often occurs in flocks which are of one sex only but are usually accompanied by other seed eaters. In winter they roam the countryside feeding on ploughed fields and stubble and are often found in woodland. At that time of year they often roost communally with other seed-eaters, particularly Bramblings (*Fringilla montifringilla*), Greenfinches (*Carduelis chloris*), and House Sparrows (*Passer domesticus*).

The contact call is a 'pink, pink', very similar to that of the Great Tit (*Parus major*). Other calls used are a repeated 'wheet' or 'tsit'. In flight it calls with a soft 'tsip'. The male sings his short but cheerful little song between February and July. It normally consists of a descending scale finishing in a 'too-ee-oo' but varies considerably between districts.

The female usually constructs a very neat nest of moss interwoven with lichens, grass and rootlets. The cup is lined with hair and sometimes feathers. Four or five eggs are laid in the single clutch produced each year. They are a pale brown with brownish-purple speckles and smudged spots. Occasionally the base colour is more pale blue than brown.

Brambling *Fringilla montifringilla*
Family: Fringillidae   145 mm

The Brambling occurs throughout Europe in varying numbers at different times of the year. Its main breeding areas are in Scandinavia and European Russia and it migrates south and westwards into southern Europe for the winter. Autumn migration takes place towards the end of September when huge flocks are often seen heading south. They remain highly gregarious throughout the winter and accompany Chaffinches (*Fringilla coelebs*) and House Sparrows (*Passer domesticus*) to feed on stubble fields and in beech-woods and to roost in rhododendrons.

They also feed on the seeds of birch and alder and on the berries of mountain-ash but during the breeding season they become insectivorous when feeding young.

Its nesting habitat is in birches or on the fringes of coniferous woodland and in scrub beyond the tree-line in the far north.

The nest, usually about 2 m from the ground and built on a foundation of grasses consists of moss, fine grasses and rootlets and is decorated with pieces of birch bark and lichens. The lining is of feathers, down and hair. Externally it looks like a large Chaffinch's nest. The five or six eggs are pale blue-brown with blotches, streaks and spots of dark brown, slightly darker than those on Chaffinches' eggs.

Bramblings can easily be distinguished by their conspicuous, narrow white rump particularly when amongst mixed flocks of seed-eating birds.

The male has orange-buff shoulder patches and breast as in the top picture. In winter the head and mantle of the male is brownish flecked with black but in the spring this changes to solid black in the adult.

The Bullfinch (*Pyrrhula pyrrhula*) which also has a black head and white rump is distinguished by having bright pink underparts.

The female, as in the bottom picture, can be confused with the female Chaffinch but the plumage is paler and more buff. The breast is orange-buff and there are no white shoulder patches.

Bramblings have brown cleft-shape tails and pale brown legs. The bill is yellow in winter turning to blue-grey in the spring.

It hops and walks on the ground and has an undulating flight. The flight-call is a 'tchucc-tchucc' and the call most often heard is a high-pitched 'tsweep'.

The song, very much like that of the Greenfinch (*Carduelis chloris*) is a monotonous, drawn-out and often repeated 'dzweee'.

148

Greenfinch *Carduelis chloris*

Family: Fringillidae 150 mm

Common throughout Europe apart from northern Scandinavia, it is a partial migrant, with birds moving south and west for the winter. Wintering flocks, associate with other small seed-eating birds roaming the countryside to feed on stubble and wasteland and often roosting communally in evergreen shrubs. They are regular visitors to country and suburban gardens, where we often see them copying the tits by hanging on nut feeders.

Even during the breeding season it remains sociable and several nests can often be found close together. Nests are found in many situations, including hedgerows and small trees and especially in ivy and other creepers. A foundation of small twigs support a structure of interwoven grass, moss and wool; the lining is usually fine roots or hair. Generally two and often three broods are attempted. The four to six eggs are from buffish to pale blue with a few brownish spots and streaks.

Call notes vary from a typical finch-like 'tsoeet' or a repeated 'jup, jup' to the nasal 'dsweee'. The song is composed of twittering sounds intermixed with call notes.

The female is greyer and not so bright, with less (often much less) yellow in the wings and tail than the male illustrated.

Siskin *Carduelis spinus*

Family: Fringillidae 120 mm

The Siskin is mainly confined to Ireland, Scotland, central and north-east Europe, Sweden, southern Norway and areas of Italy and southern France. A southward and westward movement of northern birds occurs in autumn.

Its preferred habitat is coniferous woodland but birch and alder are also favourites in winter. It feeds mainly on birch and alder seeds, but also on thistles and other seeding wayside plants. It sometimes takes small berries and is coming increasingly to garden peanut feeders in late winter.

The male, shown in the right-hand picture, is brighter than the female and has a black chin and crown. The female, on the left, is similar to a juvenile, being more greyish with heavier streaking of the underparts and lacking the black on the head. Bill and legs are brown.

It hops on the ground and has a bounding finch-like flight. Its calls vary from a persistent twittering to a 'tsooee' and a high-pitched 'tsy-zing'.

The nest of mosses and thin twigs is usually at the tip of a branch high in a coniferous tree. The lining is of hairs and feathers. Four or five white eggs spotted red and pale brown are laid.

Goldfinch *Carduelis carduelis*

Family: Fringillidae

120 mm

A familiar bird of large gardens and orchards during the spring and summer, the Goldfinch is fairly common throughout Europe apart from northern Scandinavia, northern Scotland and Iceland. It is a partial migrant, many birds moving south for the winter.

It is the only small European bird with a scarlet face and black and white head. Its wings are boldly marked with black and golden yellow and its cleft tail is black and white. The mantle is a pale tawny brown merging into a white rump. The sexes are very similar.

Juveniles lack the brightly coloured head, all the upper parts being a grey-buff mixture spotted and streaked with brown. Legs and bill are a pale flesh colour.

When on the ground the bird hops. The flight is undulating and from side to side as if dancing. In autumn and winter it tends to be gregarious, feeding in small groups, often with Redpolls (*Acanthis flammea*), in birch and alder trees. It is a seed-eater and can often be seen during the winter foraging with other finches on stubble fields. Other favourite foods are the 'downy' heads of seeding thistles, burdock and other tall weeds. Young birds are fed on insects at first and are weaned on to semi-digested seed by the parents.

The Goldfinch's unmistakable flight call is a fluid 'tswitt-witt-witt-witt'. The song is a twittering variation of the flight call and is very 'canary-like'.

Nesting usually takes place in trees near the outer tips of the branches (where the nest is often quite inaccessible), but sometimes bushes or hedges are used. A favourite place seems to be in fruit trees.

The small neat nest is constructed from grasses, rootlets and wool with a lining of fine wool and sometimes hair. In parts of Europe leaves and even pine needles are used in the main structure. The five or six very pale blue eggs are spotted and streaked with pale grey and red-brown markings.

Twite *Acanthis flavirostris*
Family: Fringillidae   135 mm

The Twite occurs mainly in western Europe breeding in Scandinavia and northern Britain. It is a partial migrant with northerly birds moving south to winter in central parts of Europe.

Its main breeding habitat is on moorland or rough grassland and hill slopes. The area is usually heather, bracken or grass remote from scrub or woodland. Occasionally they choose to nest in remote open lowland areas.

In winter some birds remain in their breeding areas but most move to coastal districts where they roam in flocks, often with other finches feeding in fields, along sea walls and on saltmarshes.

The sexes are alike, being mainly pale brown above with brown and black streaks. The throat is a warm buff and underparts buff with brown streaks. The rump is a pinkish brown in the male and buff streaked with black in the female. The cleft tail is brown and the legs dark brown.

It is very similar to juvenile and female Linnets (*Acanthis cannabina*) and Redpolls (*Acanthis flammea*) but is distinguished by its bill, light yellow in winter and greyish yellow in summer. It also differs from the Linnet in having less white in the wings and tail and darker upper parts. Unlike the Redpoll it has no black chin, no red on the crown and it has a longer tail.

The flight is undulating and on the ground it hops. When it is in flight it twitters almost continuously. Its main call, also uttered in flight, is a 'twa-it' and sometimes a 'chweet'.

The song, similar to the Linnet's, is a slow musical twitter.

The nest is usually in heather but often well-hidden crevices in banks or walls or even on the ground are used. A small cup-shaped nest is built of twigs, grass stems and moss and lined with wool and oddments of hair and feathers. A normal clutch of eggs is five or six. They are pale blue streaked and spotted with dark brown markings. Occasionally there are two broods per season.

Linnet *Acanthis cannabina*

Family: Fringillidae

135 mm

The Linnet is a partial migrant breeding throughout Europe apart from in Iceland and northern Scandinavia. Northern populations move south and westward to winter in southern and central Europe.

The top picture shows the male. He has warm brown upper parts streaked darker and buff underparts streaked with brown. The breast is tinged pink. During the breeding season the head is greyish with a crimson forehead. The forked tail is brown and edged with white and the brown wings show a prominent whitish wing patch in flight or at rest.

The female, as in the lower picture, is more streaked and lacks the pink and crimson colouring.

They have pinkish legs and dark brown bills.

They can always be distinguished from similar birds like the Redpoll (*Acanthis flammea*) and Twite (*Acanthis flavirostris*) by their warmer brown upper parts. They also lack the black chin of the Redpoll and the yellow bill of the Twite.

In flight they can be distinguished by the prominent white sides to the tail. The flight is markedly undulating and dancing from side to side. On the ground they hop.

Being highly gregarious at all times, they often nest colonially but generally solitarily. In winter they often flock with other seed-eaters to feed.

In flight they often call with a rapid twitter. They also use the typical finch-call 'tsooeet'. The song, usually performed from the top of a bush or tree, and sometimes in chorus with other Linnets is a varied musical twittering.

The preferred habitat in winter is on stubbles, wasteland, marshes and rough areas near the coast, but in the breeding season they favour heathland and gorse-covered commons and any rough areas with scattered bushes and hedges. In some areas they prefer heather and marram grass.

Nest sites vary from the top of the bushes about 4 m from the ground to brambles, young conifers and even vegetable fields. Sometimes walls and banks are used and occasionally the nest is on the ground amongst marram grass. The nest is generally of grasses and plant stalks and sometimes includes twigs and moss. A lining of wool, hair or feathers is used.

The four to six eggs are pale blue, spotted and streaked with dark brown. Two broods are usual, with occasionally a third.

Redpoll *Acanthis flammea*

Family: Fringillidae   130 mm

The Redpoll is more widely distributed over Europe during the winter months. At other times it is mainly confined to the mountainous and hilly country of central Europe, the British Isles, northern Scandinavia and parts of Iceland.

The preferred habitats are very diverse, including arctic tundra, rock outcrops well above the tree line in mountainous districts, and deciduous forest in the north, as well as alder, willow, and birch scrub in the south.

The British and Alpine race (Lesser Redpoll, *Acanthis flammea cabaret*) is shown in the upper picture. It is the smallest and is more brown with streaked upper parts and faint wing bar. The lower picture is of the Continental race (Mealy Redpoll, *A. f. flammea*). It is slightly larger and paler and has a clearer whiter wing bar and paler rump. Other races occurring in Europe are the Greenland race (Greater Redpoll, *A. f. rostrata*), which is larger still and darker, and the Arctic Redpoll (*A. hornemanni*), which has much whiter and less streaked underparts than any of the other races.

Redpolls are distinguished from other small brown finches by the blackish chin. Adults have a bright red forehead. The body plumage is brownish with darker streaking. During the breeding season males develop a brighter pinkish breast and rump. Juveniles' plumage shows no signs of red or pink. The legs are brown and the bill yellowish. The upper picture of a courting display shows the male on the right. The flight is undulating and very similar to the Goldfinch (*Carduelis carduelis*).

The characteristic high-pitched call 'chuch-uch-uch' is uttered mainly in flight. Often a call 'tiu-tiu-tiu' is given and sometimes a finch-like 'tsooeet'.

The trilling song consists of a series of vibrating notes punctuated by the flight calls and is either performed from high in a tree or during display when it flies in wide circles high in the air.

The sociable nature of this bird continues into the breeding season when colonial nesting often occurs. Nesting takes place in small trees and bushes, particularly birch, alder, willow, hawthorn or juniper. Nests are usually found from one to four metres above the ground.

The five or six eggs are pale blue spotted red and brown at one end and are laid in a small cup-shaped nest, built of fine twigs, grass and moss. The lining is usually of hair and fluffy plant fibres.

The Redpoll is gregarious in winter, roaming the countryside in search of seeds.

Bullfinch *Pyrrhula pyrrhula*

Family: Fringillidae 150 mm

The breeding range of the Bullfinch covers much of Europe. It is absent from Iceland, northern Scandinavia, southern Iberia and parts of the Mediterranean coast, and areas in the south-east. In central and southern Europe it is mainly resident but more northerly populations migrate south for the winter.

In the north it is found mainly in coniferous woodland with dense undergrowth but further south it favours all types of woodland, thickets, hedgerows, country gardens and orchards.

It is a well-known pest in fruit-growing areas where, in early spring, they systematically strip the buds from fruit trees. At other times they feed on seeds and berries.

The male, as shown in the top picture, is identified by the bright pink cheeks and underparts, blue-grey mantle, black cap and chin and black wings and tail. He has a conspicuous white rump, particularly when flying away, and a white wing-bar.

The female, as in the bottom picture, and the juvenile have similar black and white markings but the upper parts are grey-brown and the underparts pinky brown.

The stubby bill is black and the legs brown.

The northern European race (*P. p. pyrrhula*) is discernibly larger and brighter than the British race (*P. p. nesa*).

The usual calls are a soft but penetrating low piping: 'tioo' or 'wheep'. The very feeble song is a mixture of warbling, creaking and piping notes.

The flight is undulating and when on the ground it hops.

Nesting often starts in early April when a site is chosen in a thick evergreen bush or a tree. In some areas, however, brambles, hawthorn or even heather is used. A base is constructed of twigs and then a cup is formed with dark coloured rootlets, lichen and hair.

Four to six eggs are laid. They are greenish blue in colour and have dark brown spots and streaks at the fat end. Two broods per year are normally attempted.

Hawfinch *Coccothraustes coccothraustes*

Family: Fringillidae

170 mm

The Hawfinch is well distributed in central and eastern Europe but is seldom seen in the northern and western parts of the British Isles, Iceland, Spain or Scandinavia apart from an area in the south-east. North-easterly birds tend to move south-westwards to central and southern Europe for the winter. It is found mainly in woodland, particularly where beech and hornbeam are present but also in orchards, parks and gardens where there are mature trees.

The Hawfinch is very wary and secretive, flying off at the least disturbance. It is easily identified by its huge bill and thick neck. Its wings are blue-black with a huge white wing bar and the stubby tail is tipped with white. These white markings aid identification when the bird is flying away. The plumage on the back and crown is chestnut-brown in the male with a greyish nape; underparts are a pinkish buff and the lores and chin are black. The legs are flesh-brown and the bill is grey-blue. In winter the bill becomes a pale yellow and the plumage takes on a paler, more drab appearance. Females are paler than males and have a more buffish crown. Juveniles are duller with plumage barred brown and a pale yellow chin.

The bounding flight is fairly fast. On the ground it hops, and walks in an upright stance. The bill is well adapted for feeding on all sorts of seeds and nuts but it does consume insects, often catching them on the wing. Its loud call note 'tick-tick-it' or just 'tick' is often uttered in flight; another call is a thin 'tseep'. The song is very feeble and seldom heard.

Early in May a cup-shaped nest is constructed in the branches of deciduous trees, sometimes very low but sometimes in the tree top. The birds often build in a small, scattered colony in fruit trees. A thick base of sticks supports a structure of grass, stalks and rootlets, the cup being lined with hair. The five or six dirty white eggs are speckled and streaked with black and grey.

In the autumn Hawfinches congregate in small flocks roaming woodland in search of fallen seeds.

162

House Sparrow *Passer domesticus*
Family: Passeridae 150 mm

The House Sparrow is one of our commonest birds, mainly resident throughout Europe apart from Iceland and the northern-most part of Scandinavia. The brighter coloured Italian Sparrow (*P. d. italiae*), once considered as a subspecies and now regarded only as a race, occurs in Italy and Crete.

The upper parts are brown with darker streaks and underparts are buffish. The male, as in the left-hand picture, has a grey crown and rump and a black chin and throat, unlike the Tree Sparrow (*Passer montanus*) which has a brown crown and a black spot on the ear coverts. The female, in the right-hand picture, and juvenile have no distinctive markings, being dull brown above and dirty buff below.

The robust bill is horn coloured and the legs pale brown.

It is highly gregarious.

The nest is generally in a cavity in a building but is sometimes built high in thick hedges and often in nest-boxes provided for other birds. The nest of grasses is lined with feathers. The three to six eggs are whitish with grey and brown spots and blotches. As many as four broods are attempted each year.

Tree Sparrow *Passer montanus*

Family: Passeridae   145 mm

The Tree Sparrow is quite widespread in Europe. Northern and eastern populations tend to be migratory, wintering in southern Europe.

It is found from the tundra of the north to the gardens of houses in the south where there are cavities in which to roost and nest, such as quarries, pollard willows or haystacks. They often use nest-boxes.

The nest, normally in a crevice, but occasionally a flask-shaped affair in a thick bush, is built of grasses and moss and lined with feathers. The four to six off-white eggs have spots and blotches of brown and grey. Two or more broods per year are normal. Quite often Tree Sparrows are colonial nesters.

They are similar to male House Sparrows (*Passer domesticus*) but are distinguished by the chocolate-brown crown and yellowish-brown rump, a conspicuous black mark on the white ear coverts and a black bib. The upper parts are chestnut with darker streaks and underparts a pale buffish grey. The legs are pale brown and bill blackish.

The distinctive flight calls are 'teck-teck' and a ringing 'chip-chup'.

Starling *Sturnus vulgaris*

Family: Sturnidae 215 mm

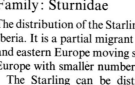

The distribution of the Starling covers most of Europe apart from Iberia. It is a partial migrant with populations from Scandinavia and eastern Europe moving south and west to winter in southern Europe with smaller numbers continuing into North Africa.

The Starling can be distinguished by its mottled blackish plumage, short tail, long sharp bill and pointed wings. Its movements are a characteristic walking with a bustling gait and in flight it can be recognised by fast wingbeats interspersed with frequent glides.

The adults' plumage as in the picture is blackish with purple and bronze-green iridescence. The mottled appearance becomes more obvious in the winter especially in females and juveniles. Juveniles are dull brown with a paler throat and become darker in the late autumn. Adults have yellow bills in the summer becoming brownish in winter like the juveniles. The legs are a warm brown.

When feeding it tends to be quarrelsome and noisy. Its main call is a raucous drawn-out 'tcheer' but it also squawks. The song uttered from a prominent perch is a conglomeration of squeaks, whistles, vibrating sounds, trills and rattles with no apparent pattern.

It is a very good mimic and this often accounts for some species being 'heard' in abnormal situations. It is always wise to check and be certain that the sound does not come from a Starling.

When not breeding it is extremely gregarious. In the autumn and winter huge flocks congregate at dusk to roost on city buildings or in woodland or reed-beds. It regularly flocks with Rooks (*Corvus frugilegus*), Jackdaws (*Corvus monedula*) and Lapwings (*Vanellus vanellus*) to feed. Throughout the year Starlings frequent rubbish tips in large numbers, often accompanied by gulls. They can be found almost anywhere in open country apart from isolated moorland but seem to favour the proximity of human habitation from isolated houses to the centre of large cities.

They nest almost exclusively in cavities: the site may be in the walls or roof space of a building, in a tree or cliff face or in the old enclosed nest of some other bird. In barren areas they often use holes in the ground. They take readily to nest-boxes. The untidy nest is a collection of straw and grasses and is lined with feathers or other soft material available locally.

From four to seven pale blue eggs are laid and sometimes two broods are attempted.

Jay *Garrulus glandarius*
Family: Corvidae   340 mm

Well distributed throughout most of Europe apart from northern Scandinavia and Scotland and Iceland. It is a partial migrant in the northern part of the range. The Jay's body plumage is a pinkish brown with a black tail and a white rump which is very conspicuous in flight. The wings are black and white with a beautiful blue and black barred wing patch. The crown feathers are white flecked with black and they are often raised as a crest in display. The eyes are noticeably pale, the legs are brownish and the thick bill is black. Both sexes have like plumage.

The Jay frequents deciduous and mixed woodland with thick undergrowth, particularly where oak predominates, but it is also found in thickets, young plantations, orchards and large gardens.

During the winter they gather in small flocks to roam the countryside. In early springtime and in autumn when acorns are abundant larger congregations often occur.

It is very wary, flying off and calling when approached by humans. The call is a harsh, penetrating 'shraaak, shraaak', but other quieter mewing and clucking noises are made. When nesting, however, it remains fairly quiet.

It is omnivorous, taking insects, seeds and small animals, and is well known for its liking of other birds' eggs.

Nesting occurs from mid-April in fairly secluded woodland. A cup-shaped nest is constructed of small twigs and lined with fine roots or hair. It is usually situated in a fork, high in a young tree or bush. In larger trees the nest is often near the trunk.

A single clutch of from five to seven eggs is usually laid. They are a dark buff finely mottled with pale brown and often having black streakings and hair lines at the thick end.

Jay in flight – note the white rump

168

Magpie *Pica pica*
Family: Corvidae   260 mm

The Magpie is a resident preferring open country with trees and large bushes but it occasionally comes close to human habitation. It is extremely shy and wary and if approached will soon fly away uttering its raucous, chuckling call, a 'chak-chak-chak-chak'. During the breeding season it makes various piping and chuckling noises.

It is easily identified by its pied appearance and long tail. Most of the plumage is black with green-blue or purple sheen. The belly, flanks and scapulars are white. The bill and legs are black.

It is omnivorous. It walks and hops when on the ground and has a weak flight. In the winter it roams around in small flocks but larger numbers often occur during spring and at roosts.

The nest is normally high in a bush or isolated tree, but in some places it is built very low in brambles or long heather. It is of twigs plastered inside with mud and lined with fine roots, grass or hair. A canopy of thorny twigs usually covers the whole nest. The five to seven eggs are greenish mottled with grey-green spots.

Jackdaw *Corvus monedula*

Family: Corvidae   330 mm

The Jackdaw is a partial migrant, distributed throughout Europe apart from Iceland and northern Scandinavia. Northern populations winter in western and central Europe.

It is the only predominantly black bird with a grey nape, shoulders and ear coverts. The underparts are dark grey, the eye a pearl-grey, and the bill and legs black. It is smaller than all similar birds in the Crow family and has a much shorter bill.

Its movement on the ground and in flight is faster than those of the larger black crows. It is highly gregarious even nesting communally and regularly associating with Rooks (*Corvus frugilegus*). Its breeding habitat varies from old buildings in the centres of towns to cliffs, quarries and parkland with old trees.

The nest is normally in some cavity, and is mainly of twigs with oddments of rubbish such as paper and grasses. A thin lining of wool or hair is usually present.

Four to six light blue-green eggs with brown spots and streaks are laid.

The calls are a clear repeated 'chack' and during the breeding season various chattering sounds and a brief 'chya'.

171

Rook *Corvus frugilegus*

Family: Corvidae   460 mm

The Rook is a partial migrant breeding mainly in central Europe, with the more northerly populations tending to move south and west for the winter. In the west of the range winter movements are much more local.

The plumage is predominantly black with a purplish iridescence. The adults are easily distinguished from other Crows by their bare greyish-white skin patch around the base of the bill. The bill is greyish black and more slender and pointed than in other Crows. The thighs are well feathered, giving an appearance of 'baggy' trousers. The legs are black.

Rooks are much bigger and lack the grey nape of the Jackdaw (*Corvus monedula*). The Raven (*Corvus corax*) is larger still and has a huge bill in comparison.

Juveniles have duller plumage and a fully feathered face and can be confused with the Carrion Crow (*Corvus corone*) apart from the more slender bill.

The flight is direct and rather laboured but is faster and with more regular wingbeats than the Carrion Crow. It walks when on the ground.

At all times of the year it is highly gregarious, nesting communally in trees, often in the neighbourhood of nesting Jackdaws. Only very occasionally do odd pairs nest away from a 'rookery'.

It prefers agricultural land with scattered trees and moves around in flocks searching the fields for leatherjackets and cockchafers. Although its main diet is insects and worms, it does consume some seed. In summer it also feeds on uncultivated land and occasionally along the sea-shore.

Rookeries are usually situated in the tallest trees in the district and may be on tree-clad agricultural land or even in trees in small towns. They are seldom in areas of heavy afforestation. The size of the rookery varies from a few to hundreds of pairs.

The nests, usually amongst the higher branches are made almost entirely of twigs, but a lining of grass, leaves and moss and sometimes wool and feathers is frequently used.

Egg laying starts as early as the end of March and from four to six eggs are laid in a single clutch each year. The eggs are pale green with heavy spotting and blotching of grey and brown.

The Rook has many calls from a 'Raven-like' croaking to a higher-pitched 'ki-oor' similar to a gull. Its main calls are a 'kaw' or 'kaaa', less harsh but more prolonged than the call of the Carrion Crow.

Rook – note the shaggy 'trousers' and bare face patch

Carrion Crow

Species Index

Vernacular English names are printed in bold type. Scientific names are in italics. The figures in bold type refer to the pages on which the main species are described. The other figures refer to the descriptive text pages.

174

Societies

For those interested in birds, membership of an ornithological society can be a source of pleasure and knowledge, and will be of help in the protection and conservation of wild birds.

In the United Kingdom there are numerous local societies and naturalists' trusts. There are also two national organisations which between them cater for a wide range of ornithological interests. They are the Royal Society for the Protection of Birds and the British Trust for Ornithology.

The Royal Society for the Protection of Birds concerns itself with the protection of all species of wild British birds. Its operations cover many aspects of conservation including the acquisition and running of reserves, education and conservation planning. Other facets of its work include law enforcement, scientific research, the production of films and publications about birds and a farming and wildlife advisory service.

The Young Ornithologists' Club is the junior section of the R.S.P.B. catering for young people up to the age of fifteen. Their interest is promoted through local outings, holiday courses and their own magazine.

Details of membership can be obtained from:
The Royal Society for the Protection of Birds
The Lodge
Sandy
Bedfordshire
SG19 2DL
England

The British Trust for Ornithology concerns itself with identifying the influences which affect birdlife to provide the facts to guide conservation where it is most effective. All B.T.O. members are encouraged to participate in many types of fieldwork including censuses and surveys, nest records scheme, bird ringing and other special inquiries.

Details of membership can be obtained from:
The British Trust for Ornithology
Beech Grove
Tring
Hertfordshire
HP23 5NR
England